Spiritual Identity Fraud

Restoring God's Sons and Daughters

Jonathan S. Potter

…"I will be a Father to you, And you shall be

My sons and daughters,

Says the LORD Almighty."

(2 Corinthians 6:18)

Foreword

By J. Lee Grady

T homas Dewar, the famous Scottish whiskey baron who died in 1930, once said: "An honest confession is good for the soul, but bad for the reputation." Many men from Dewar's generation lived by that maxim. They knew that Christianity taught the importance of confession, but they decided to hide their sins and mistakes in order to get ahead in the business world.

The same is true today for the majority of men. We don't really know how to be honest. We learn at an early age to build fortresses of macho pride. We put on body armor and pretend to be tough. We never allow anyone to see our weaknesses.

And thus we have created the dysfunctional American male. He looks good on the outside—in fact he may spend a lot of time in the gym working on his abs. He reads GQ to learn what to wear and how to perform in bed. All his goals center on how to beat the other guy in business or sports. But when he is ready to go to sleep at night he is plagued by nagging guilt and loneliness.

I wish I could say this is only true for men outside the church. But today, the dysfunctional American male is often sitting in a pew listening to a sermon but suffering in silence. Most Christian men avoid honest confession. We've learned to "suit up" for church by putting on masks and religious fronts— knowing all along that we aren't what we say we are.

Men have struggled with this dilemma ever since Adam sinned in the Garden of Eden and went looking for some leaves to cover his nakedness. I call it the Great Cover-up. Guys are particularly skilled at inventing ways to hide their true selves!

You know the story from the book of Genesis. After Adam created a primitive jock strap made of fig leaves, God confronted him by saying: "Who told you that you were naked?

Have you eaten from the tree of which I commanded you not to eat?" (Gen. 3:11). In true male form, Adam blamed his wife—again masking the sad truth that he had disobeyed God and was unwilling to take responsibility for his actions.

In the end of that story, the Bible reveals that the withering fig leaves were not acceptable clothes for Adam or Eve. "The Lord God made garments of skin for Adam and his wife, and clothed them" (3:21).

This was the first indication in Scripture that sin would require bloodshed. The fact that an animal had to die to clothe the ancestors of the human race clearly foreshadowed the day when Jesus Christ, the only begotten Son of God, would die on a crude cross so that we could be forgiven and restored to fellowship with the Father.

The blood of Jesus is the only thing that can truly forgive us for our past sins and give us power to live the way God intended. We don't need a flimsy cover-up. We need His covering!

Men today are looking for all kinds of ways to cover their guilt: Many guys turn to the numbing influence of alcohol or drugs; others try sex; still others fill their time with sports or video games so they don't have to think about eternal realities. And many church-going men cover themselves with religion without fully knowing the power of Christ's forgiveness.

This is the message of the book you are holding in your hands. I encourage you to read it carefully.

What I love about Jon Potter is his honesty. Contrary to Thomas Dewar, Jon doesn't care about his reputation. He is willing to admit the dark secrets of his past—including a horrific childhood experience with sexual molestation. I don't know many guys who are man enough to admit they were "messed with" when they were boys. Most of us are afraid to bring such dirty secrets into the open; we think others might judge us or snicker behind our backs. Personally, I think Jon Potter is a stronger and better man for baring his soul.

Had Jon kept his secret hidden, he would have only known the covering of fig leaves. But because he was brutally honest about his pain—and the shame of the other sinful habits he struggled with—he traded his fig leaves for the blood of Jesus. And he discovered the deep forgiveness that is offered to all of us.

The Bible tells us an amazing truth in James 5:16: "Therefore confess your sins to one another, and pray for one another so that you may be healed." Notice that confession in this passage is not just directed toward God; it requires transparency with others. I have learned over the years that if I want real breakthrough over temptation, it is not enough for me to talk to God about it. He wants me to humble myself and admit my weakness to my brother.

Why is that? Simply because open confession requires genuine humility. When we admit our flaws and mistakes to others, God deals a death blow to our pride—which is the root of all our sins and addictions. And when pride is gone, God's grace can move in and help you.

I believe Jon Potter's honest book can start a revolution—a revolution of honesty. It is time for all of us to come out of hiding. And I believe this significant book will help you make the journey toward true healing.

J. Lee Grady, Author

10 Lies the Church Tells Women

25 Tough Questions About Women and the Church

The Holy Spirit Is Not for Sale

10 Lies Men Believe

Praise for Spiritual Identity Fraud!

"Forfeited victory. Anemic grace. Disillusioned believers. Finally there is an answer…From start to finish, Jon has identified and dismantled the underlying barrier that has enslaved and disinherited so many believers in the Family of God–the disconnected and disillusioned heart.

It is shocking to feel the tug on the surface of your spirit as Jon gently peels back the protective veneer of religiosity and pride that has enslaved so many to a life of emptiness and loss. Then, using a laugh-out-loud humor, raw candor, profound simplicity and Scriptural precision, this amazing journey will create an inescapable impact on your mind and heart as you rediscover a place called *home*!

Are you looking for that elusive, missing '*something*' that will finally bring rest, balance and vision to your life? You've found it…This is not just another Christian book. It is one of gut-level honesty and definitive answers established on proven truths! This book will absolutely revolutionize every reader's heart."

Pastor Scott Thomas, Senior Pastor
Without Walls Central Church
Lakeland, Florida

My friend and fellow father has done it again…With clarity beyond his young years, Jon Potter reveals the truth that God is still looking for His kids. All of us have heard all our lives that we all must, even the adults, have childlike faith. Jesus said, "suffer the *children* to come unto me"…not the men or women. Men and women of God…must become as a Child. We must reconnect to and recommit our Childlike faith. Pastor Jon is right, God is still looking for His kids.

Kevin D. Brooks, State Representative
Tennessee – 24th District

David knew how blessed we were to be able to call our Heavenly Father, our 'Abba Daddy' when he stated, 'What is man that thou art mindful of him or the Son of Man that thou visitest him.' In 'Spiritual Identity Fraud...Restoring God's Sons and Daughters,' Jon draws the picture very clearly how we can trust our Father to be who He says He is.

That is the good news, but the challenging news is that we have a responsibility also. There comes a time to 'put away childish things' and to become the men and women that He designed us to be. The Word says, 'Though He was a Son, yet learned He obedience through the things that He suffered." (Hebrews 5:8) That is the theme of this astounding book, simply because the author, Jon Potter, has become the passionate, obedient, and anointed Son of God that he is, simply through his suffering, hurt, pain, disappointment and courage to keep pressing on toward the prize. This book will challenge, provoke, and inspire you to go beyond the status-quo and to dare to follow God's plan.

Judy Jacobs, Psalmist, Author, Co-Pastor
His Song Ministries, Mentor

Jonathan Potter has opened his life and heart for all to see how he has come to know the grace of God expressed through "sonship." He draws insights from Scripture and connects them to the plight of modern western manhood providing a trustworthy bridge from a life of defeat to a life of hope and joy. This is one of those serious 'must-reads' for people seeking to be a more serious disciple of Jesus Christ!

Dr. Doug Beacham, Director of World Missions

International Pentecostal Holiness Church

Oklahoma City, Oklahoma

Jon shares that he heard in his spirit that God has called him to be a CHILD of God and NOT a man of God. This simple but hidden truth was not only profound to Jon, but to me as well. This book speaks truth into our sometimes confused theology and reminds us of who we are in Christ. I recommend it to anyone seeking a deeper revelation of our Heavenly Father!

Greg Long, Avalon

Contemporary Christian Recording Artist

Such an awesome book. I have been challenged to be the best possible father to my children based on God's greatest example to me as my Heavenly Father. It's definitely a must read for all homes. I love it!

Jamie Tuttle, Co-founder, His Song Ministries

Senior Pastor, Dwelling Place Church International, Cleveland, TN

Becoming who God has really called us to be is a quest of incredible importance. In my own life, I have often answered the question of who God has called me to be with a list of roles

I filled such as husband, father, journalist and businessman. I am so grateful that my friend Jon Potter has sought God's word for the true answer. Jon is a man I respect, and a minister I admire. His passion and anointing are evident every time he opens his mouth to preach or picks up a pen to write. Thanks, Jon, for tackling a subject we all struggle with, our identity.

David Lamb, NBC Anchor and TV Personality
Birmingham, Alabama

Honor

My deepest honor to…

My precious father and mother, Rev. and Mrs. James Wesley Potter. By your lives, you consistently demonstrated the great commission. Mom - you taught and daily mentored me in how to love God and his eternal word. Dad - through your selfless lifestyle, you showed me how to love my neighbor as myself. I am eternally grateful for all you have imparted into my life.

My family. Jay and Melissa; Janna and Greg. We have grown from siblings and in-laws into true friends. Thank you for your belief in me. I cherish you. To Art, Betty, Greg, Holly and all the Hodge extended family, thank you for accepting me. I have never felt *anything* less than loved by you. I love you all.

Our covenant friends. Jamie, Judy; Jim, Kathy; Joe, Sharon; Richard, Shelly; and Chuck and Mel. Thanks for believing in us when no one else did. We are connected forever!

Steve and Deena Franklin. You were my first *extended* spiritual parents beyond my childhood. You believed in me and enabled me to leave God's permissive will and step into my destiny. I have never seen faith like yours or precious Bryant's. I love you both. Steve, I am forever indebted to your investment in me…you are a champion of champions. www.sfmin. com

The father-figures and "brothers" who have touched my life. Charles Rogers, Chris Lowder, John Mills, Lonnie Carter, Mike Weigert, Art Hodge, Danny Murray, Al Yother, Richard Randolph, Danny Stone, Chris Allen, Stan Tuttle, Francois Fineberg, Dr. Finley McCrae, and Lee Grady. You all have poured your love, correction, instruction and friendship into who I am. I am a better man because of you.

My precious spiritual "mothers" who have nurtured and prayed for God to make my life count. Cathy Lowder, Gail Mills, Patti Yother, Paige Jackson, Betty McCrae, Jean Carraway, Laura Dee Wood, Linda Myers, and Sylvia Gunter.

You all have touched my heart with your spiritual fingerprints. Thank you for being a "mom" and a *mother* when I needed one!

Our Tuesday prayer group. Yaaay we did it! For nearly seven years we have touched the hem of his garment and gone out into the deep places in God. Thank you, thank you, thank you, for allowing me to make mistakes as we learn to rightly divide the Word of Truth.

My editorial help. Jan Coleman and Dr. Frank Tunstall. Jan, you took this "meal" I was trying to serve on a paltry paper plate and placed it on fine china. Thank you is not enough. You truly are "brilliance on demand!" www.jancoleman.com. To Dr. Frank Tunstall. Your scriptural insight and correction were so relevant and needed. I thank you for loving me enough to speak the truth and critique without family bias.

Every friend and partner of Jon Potter Ministries who's financial gifts made this work, and makes our livelihood, possible. May God credit your spiritual account with an abundant return for every dollar given. We thank God upon every remembrance of you!

Dedications

I dedicate this book to my three amazing children, Elliott, Barrett, and Kelsey. You have all brought me indescribable joy and have helped life make sense. I am far beyond proud and well-pleased with all of you and my heart swells with joy when I think of you. Thank you for your unconditional love when I have been less than the daddy you all deserve. I charge you all to know your true Father and daily seek the mysteries of who he is.

I dedicate this book to my wife Lisa. God smiled on me the night I met you. You believed in me first as a minister and as an author. Thanks for being my best cheerleader and best friend. Thank you for never giving up on what you saw I was and am to become. I truly do not deserve the gift of your love and your life. Let's grow old together! 143

I dedicate this book to my Lord and Savior Jesus Christ! Oh how I desire to be conformed into your image. This is the story of your workmanship in my life thus far. Thank you for giving me beauty for ashes and a thousand second chances. Please help me to live out what you have shown me and be a son worthy of your name!

He shall build a house for My name, and I will establish the

throne of his kingdom forever.

14 I will be his Father, and he shall be My son.

(2 Samuel 7:13-14)

…And he will turn

The hearts of the fathers to the children,

And the hearts of the children to their fathers…

(Malachi 4:6)

…And suddenly a voice came from heaven, saying, "This is

My beloved Son, in whom I am well pleased."

(Matthew 3:17)

…Blessed are the peacemakers, For they shall be

called sons of God.

(Matthew 5:9)

All things have been delivered to Me by My Father, and no

one knows the Son except the Father. Nor does anyone know

the Father except the Son, and the one to whom the

Son wills to reveal Him.

(Matthew 11:27-28)

… except you become as a little child, you will not enter the

Kingdom of Heaven

(Matthew 18:3)

…Adam, the son of God.

(Luke 3:38)

I will not leave you orphans; I will come to you.

(John 14:18)

For as many as are led by the Spirit of God,

these are sons of God.

(Romans 8:14)

For [the Spirit which] you have now received [is] not a spirit

of slavery to put you once more in bondage to fear, but you

have received the Spirit of adoption [the Spirit producing

sonship] in [the bliss of] which we cry, Abba (Father)!

(Romans 8:15 AMP)

…There, they shall be called sons of the living God.

(Romans 9:26)

For it was fitting for Him, for whom are all things and by whom are all things, in bringing many sons to glory, to make the captain of their salvation perfect through sufferings.

(Hebrews 2:10)

If you endure chastening, God deals with you as with sons; for what son is there whom a father does not chasten? 8 But if you are without chastening, of which all have become partakers, then you are illegitimate and not sons

(Hebrews 12:7-8)

Behold what manner of love the Father has bestowed on us, that we should be called children of God!

(1 John 3:1)

He who overcomes shall inherit all things, and I will be his God and he shall be My son.

(Revelation 21:7)

Contents

Introduction

…After all, though you should have ten thousand
teachers (guides to direct you) in Christ, *yet you do not
have many fathers*. For I became your *father* in Christ
Jesus through the glad tidings (the Gospel).
(1 Corinthians 4:15 AMP)

Over 2,000 years ago the Apostle Paul made this statement regarding spiritual fathering. Today not too much
has changed, except ten thousand teachers might now be
approaching the ten million mark. You would think we would
have improved in two millennia, yet in our world of mega ministries and global Christian media, fatherlessness is still the
scourge of most cultures. I believe this void of fathering may

be the epicenter of all of the brokenness found in the human condition.

Too often, The Body of Christ has sat idle expecting governments and social cure initiatives to effect change; however, true transformation of a person, a people, and a nation, comes about only through an intimate relationship with Abba Father. The truth is, that we will never be able to replicate the fathering that the Apostle Paul accomplished with the early Church, until we understand just who Abba is, *and who we are as his children.*

The Bible clearly tells us that God is the sovereign Lord of the universe, yet Jesus told us to address him as "Father." Paul's epistles underscore the truth that God has been raising sons and daughters for thousands of years. In Roman culture, at the time when he wrote the above words, an adopted person inherited all the rights of a legitimate child in his new family.

As his adopted children, God also raises us from spiritual infancy through our spiritually formative years and on to mature "sonship," with divine privileges as our inheritance!

In the New Testament, the phrase "sons of God" means "children of God" or "offspring." It has nothing to do with gender, but more our position in God after regeneration, and let me add, men and women are equal in worth and value to our Heavenly Father.

Four years ago on a muggy September night, God's Spirit began to speak to me about my true identity that could only found in sonship. This launched a quest that changed my life. This pursuit has been at times painful, revelatory, but ultimately, liberating beyond belief.

I learned at an early age that becoming a man is my genetic destination and responsibility; however, I have discovered that *sonship* is something altogether different and much more wonderful! Sonship and daughtership are divine *privileges*, and God has ventured our present fulfillment and eternal destiny upon it. I do know this, a faithful child in God's eyes will always become a great man or woman.

The enemy of our souls has too-long pillaged our inheritance with his subtle lies and fraudulent schemes, deceiving the Church that it's okay to live beneath our pedigree as God's children. Well, his deception has been discovered, and I say "No More!"

My hope is that this book about rediscovering who we are, and the way this process unfolded in my own life, will have the same impact for you. I pray that it will stir you to seek, probe and explore—in a new and deeper way—our relationship with

Father God, the new identity this relationship provides, and our *adult response* as his children.

Yes, his children. Our Father is still looking for his kids.

For the earnest expectation of the creation, eagerly waits

for the revealing of the sons of God.

(Romans 8:19)

Chapter 1

Living the American Mirage

Behold what manner of love the Father has bestowed on us,
that we should be called children of God.

(1 John 3:1)

In late summer of 2006, I spent a night at our at church in intense prayer. Among many other petitions, the gist of one of my sincere heart cries during those 8 hours went something like this…"Oh God, I want to be a mighty man for you. I want to be a man full of your zeal, a man filled with your power and living in your purity, a man with whom you are well-pleased."

I longed to hear from God, and as I was about to rise from the floor in our church's prayer room, I clearly heard him whisper something to my spirit that astounded and changed me forever. **"Jon, I never called you to be a man of God.** *I called you to be a child of God."*

Whoa, Lord. What in the world did you just say? I eased back down on my knees, pondering what I felt the Lord had just said to me. I waited on him, pausing to listen for his voice. The same message came to me again and again. *"I called you to be a child of God."*

My mind reeled like a spool of film in a documentary that could have been titled *Jon Potter's Life So Far.* As a young kid who day dreamed of being a great preacher like his father, I was well-aware that all the powerful ministers who stepped into the pulpit, and all sought-after evangelists on the platform, were always and forever referred to as mighty "men" and "women" of God!

After church, we would invite these ministers to our home. There in our living room, I would listen to their fantastic stories of God-sized miracles and adventures, as the percolator would bubble and the delicious aroma of Maxwell House would fill our kitchen.

To me, this title of "mighty man of God" was a distinction to strive for, the culmination of arriving at who you were cre-ated to be, and I just knew I was destined to be one...one day.

Nevertheless, God's message to me early that morning after prayer was clear. He called me to be his child. The great question I had to answer, was why would he speak sonship to my heart? What did I not understand after 30+ years of knowing him? There are more complicated answers that I could give, but I now believe what God said might distill to this: Children awaken every morning in a state of complete dependence on mom and dad to meet their needs. They have no well-thought-out solution for the day's provision and demands. They are beautifully inept to fend for even the basics needs of life, and can only hope by parental provision to survive day by day.

Isn't this condition reminiscent of Jesus' words of in Matthew 6:31-32? "So don't worry about these things, saying 'What shall we eat?' or 'What shall we drink?' or 'What shall we wear?' These things dominate the thoughts of unbelievers, but your Heavenly Father already knows your needs." (NLT)

God does not simply plop us into his family and then disappear from our daily lives, leaving us to learn to walk, talk and make sense of the world. Rather, he is an interactive parent who guides and nurtures us by his Spirit through every stage. He knows our every need, even before we ask.

When Adam fell, he and Eve were banished from the Garden and all of creation lost our pristine position. Every secular self-help book on identity, along with every philosopher who has pondered our purpose, have wittingly or otherwise sought God's plan in creating us. What they long for, what I believe we all long for, is crafted into the last line of what appears to be mundane genealogy, located in Luke chapter three, verse thirty eight.

The final verse of this third chapter says it all...*Adam was God's son*.

There you have divine sonship, plain and simple. God called Adam his son, his child, created for the Father's pleasure. This was his original intent and every damaged seed of humanity born after Adam has been a distorted simile—human and carnal—of that first divine notion.

How we have fallen from God's primary plan.

The Old Testament is peppered with the phrase "man of God." It is mentioned nearly eighty times. Yet, as I began writing this book, *it astounded me to learn that in the New Testament, we are never urged, (not even once), to become "men or women" of God!*

Does this stun you as it did me? The phrase "man of God" occurs just three times between Matthew and Revelation, and the phrase "men of God," occurs just once. Now, before I *tip a sacred cow*, let me say that I am not setting aside that this concept exists in the New Testament; however, I see much more prevalent themes, and they are all about sonship, the father heart of God and servanthood.

These themes are foundational to the Christian life. They are clearly presented and often repeated throughout all the gospels and epistles. There are an overwhelming number of references to "sonship" in God's Word, (*just some of them at the beginning of this book*.) Ephesians 1:5 says it this way, "Having predestined us to adoption as sons by Jesus Christ to Himself, according to the good pleasure of his will." Our Father determined—he decided in advance—to adopt us into his own family and bring us to himself through Jesus Christ.

He desires to restore this profound paradigm that much of Christianity may have acknowledged, but yet not fully embraced or understood. My friend, the Holy Spirit is emphatic about you assuming this identity after regeneration, when you experienced being born again.

Consider redemption's greatest accomplishment:

Jesus left Heaven as the only begotten of the Father. *He returned to Heaven as the first-born of many brethren.*

The Father is eager for us to embrace this truth. Its message is paramount to grasping our Kingdom agenda. It is such a central theme of all scripture, that the Holy Spirit weaves it through every chapter in the Bible.

It begins with Adam in Genesis, to God promising to personally father Solomon in Second Samuel, and then onward to Jesus our Savior, introduced in the gospel of Matthew. Finally, in Revelation 21:7, at the closing of his Word, God reiterates his primary intent for his Church. In this verse, he wraps up the story of redemption and places a final exclamation point concerning sonship:

"He who overcomes shall inherit all things, and I will be his God and he shall be My *son*."

Sonship may be *the* most essential tenet of all Bible doctrines. I believe it is foundational in the three stages of our spiritual metamorphoses as God's people. Through my years of study, I continually observe a pattern in the New Testament:

First, we are *positionally children of God*, and those who overcome and stand firm to the end will receive the blessings that God has promised. All those brave enough to stand up for

Christ and accept his authority over their lives will receive a bountiful inheritance.

Next, our response to this gift of sonship (and daughter-ship), is a life of *grateful service* to him as our Lord. Though seen too little in the Church, servanthood is still the heart of God and the model Jesus lived.

"I used to ask God to help me. Then I asked if I might help Him. I ended up by asking God to do His work though me." - Hudson Taylor

Finally, I believe that it is only in this paradigm of *son-ship and service*, that we gloriously transform into the Bride of Christ, awaiting the return of our bridegroom who will present us to our Father!

Oh how I wish I had known and understood this process and progression as I struggled in the formative years of my faith journey. That said, before we go any further, I'd like to take you back to my childhood for a few moments and paint a picture of who I am, and allow you to peer into my spiritual frame of reference.

Few people can endure for very long the fiery heat spewed by a Southern hellfire and brimstone Pentecostal preacher. Most wilt in their pews before the sermon is half over. Women dot their damp foreheads with a hankie and dabble at the perspiration. Men sit erect and motionless, content to allow sweat to drip down their backs. I know; I sat wide-eyed in the same pew every Sunday morning and watched the congregation *melt* as my father preached his heart out!

My dad had three other brothers who stood in pulpits and paced platforms every Sunday as well. What is fascinating to me, is that these four, with two additional siblings, were raised in a home with an alcoholic and often physically and emotionally abusive father. From my training in psychotherapy and human behavior, I know that most psychologists would have wagered against any of these boys being able to escape some form of lifestyle that repeated their childhood. Yet, such a prognosis rarely considers the power of a God-fearing, Spirit-filled, prayer-warrior mother!

My grandmother was Hannah Potter, and she could bellow prayers that made Heaven thunder and Hell quake. My father tells me that her fervent prayers were often the last thing he heard as he drifted off to sleep at night and the first sounds that awakened him each morning. She interceded and pleaded for her boys and she prevailed; ultimately, all six sons found salvation. In his book, The Powers That Be: Theology for a

New Millennium, Walter Wink said that "history belongs to the intercessors."[1] What a profound truth and mandate!

Looking back on my life, I am so grateful to have come through this spiritual matriarch, accepting the Lord into my heart at a very early age in our home. Yes, at six years old I was redeemed by God's grace, whatever that meant. It sounded fine at the time, but I had no earthly idea of the meaning and breadth of the word, *redeemed*. Only years later did those "R" words take root in me.

Redeemed. Reclaimed. Restored.

Through my formative years I struggled for my own identity, dodging too many eyes that glared into the glass-house parsonages where I grew up. Our family was often outwardly the ideal picture, expressing love and support; but sadly, we fell right into the trap that Jack Frost, founder of Shiloh Place Ministries, expounds on so well. "Many minister's homes tragically become a place where the Great Commission takes precedent over The Great Commandment." This truth resounds all too painfully for those of us who are minister's kids—PK's as we dub ourselves—and lived it.

Frost's statement inspires me to hop on my soapbox for a moment. My wife Lisa teases me when I am about to break into a spontaneous speech about my latest inspiration. "Wait," she says pretending to dash into the laundry room, "Let me get your soapbox." So here goes my first little rant for you.

The "Great Commission" is our assignment, the foundation of our work here on earth. We know that Jesus told his disciples to spread his teachings to the world and make disciples of all nations. This work should be the outward by-product of a passionate love for Christ. Yet, there is more to it than this.

Please first understand that I am not downplaying the call to save the lost, but if we are not careful, we can elevate the *call* of evangelism paramount to the *love for those who we want to reach most*. It's love that should compel us to first become and then live as his witnesses, his ambassadors. What is critical to grasp is that the work of winning the lost will never compare to the love for the lost, *especially in our immediate sphere of influence*. Where am I going with this? Lisa flat out asks me this question whenever I am on my soapbox for more than five minutes, so let me explain.

Jesus asked, "What does it profit a man to save the whole world and lose his soul?" I say, what does it profit us to go out and try to evangelize the world, if the souls of those closest to us, our family and friends, never come to a relationship with Christ?

When Jack Frost talked about the great commission, he meant that pastors, ministers and believers are often so passionate to win the world, yet inadvertently neglect their families. Their zeal to evangelize the lost, often comes at the cost of loving and winning their most immediate *world*.

We need to remember some other words of Jesus as well… *first* Jerusalem, *next* Judea, *and then*, to the uttermost parts of the earth. (Acts 1:8) Your family is your most pertinent mission field. I speak for myself when I say this. We can get so enmeshed in our church work, so busy with Kingdom business, that we forget the heart and first "commission" from the King.

Growing up as I did as a PK from the South, I was expected to be at church if the wind *cracked* the door open. We were always doing churchy things, but there were definitely times when in the middle of revivals, bake sales, and building programs, 'Jon' got lost in the crowd. My father and I had a long conversation awhile back about this and he apologetically said, "Son, I wish I had spent more time building a family than brick and mortar buildings."

This is a powerful lesson for me as a father of teenagers.

Jesus said—as the *Great Commandment*—love the Lord God with all your heart, mind and strength, and love your neighbor as yourself. (Matthew 22:37-39) This is not the great "suggestion," but a command from the Lord, a directive. And there are no closer neighbors than our spouses, our children, and families, which serve as our primary evangelism and discipleship responsibility. In the beginning, God created family to be fruitful and prosperous first. He then told Adam to *subdue the Earth*. I dare say that we do not have the right to "subdue" anything before we have loved and taught our families to "submit" to Christ Lordship. Our family is our lifelong priority.

If you are a parent, please focus on winning your kids and loved ones before anyone else. It doesn't mean trying to force feed them Scripture or bribe them to attend church. Simply model a prayer life, be an example of serving, and foster an environment that incites passion in your kids for the Kingdom. Lisa and I try to keep church and its activities in balance.

We agree with what the Apostle Paul said in Philippians that all things should be done in moderation. He speaks often about living the balanced life. And as the old adage says, we can be so Heavenly minded that we become no earthly good. After we have accomplished winning our families for Christ, *then let's go after Bangladesh.*

Soapbox time is over for now.

In the summer of my thirteenth year, my father took a pastorate in Baltimore, Maryland. This turned my world completely upside down. Moving forced me to leave everything familiar and everything Southern. Though Florence, South Carolina was considered a small town, as far as I knew, it had just about anything a young teenager could ever want or need.

It never crossed my mind that I would not graduate from West Florence High where my older brother Jay roamed the halls as a proud senior. Jay was my idol and naturally, I would also graduate from his alma mater where he tore up the football field as the starting running back of the West Florence Knights.

When Jay's coach learned we were moving to the northeast, he called my father to set up a meeting. My heart stuck in my throat like a baseball as I eavesdropped on their conversation from the kitchen. Here was Coach Cato, urging my dad to allow Jay to remain in Florence for his senior year. Jay was an amazing athlete with college scholarship potential. The loss of his talent would have been huge blow to the team. "He can live with us," the coach said. He promised my dad that he and his wife would "parent" Jay with an iron fist if needed. I watched my brother's face when he heard this option; a chance to stay in Florence with his grade school friends, and Melissa, his teenage sweetheart.

He wouldn't be forced to transfer high schools in his senior year, the biggest year of life. That would have crushed him and altered his life forever. In the end, I was the one who was crushed. My parents conceded to the coach's request, though they struggled tremendously with the decision.

They realized that letting Jay stay put in South Carolina and graduate with his classmates was the right thing for him. My younger sister, Janna, and I would relocate to Baltimore with our parents. In one momentous day, I lost my home town, my childhood friends and my hero.

When the U-Haul entered the Baltimore city limits that July of 1981, I abruptly understood what the term "culture shock" really meant. Like Dorothy when she looks around in Munchkin land and says to Toto, "We're not in Kansas anymore," I knew this was not South Carolina or anything remotely resembling my roots. No woodlands to explore, no sign of tobacco fields, no sweet tea, and as for grits – forget about it!

Skyscrapers, city buses, and billowing steam from under the streets were all foreign sights to this wide-eyed teenager. Baltimore dwarfed everything I had ever known. The population of our former town was so small that we could actually have fit into the Colt's football stadium.

Life was changing so fast I could barely keep up. Summer that year quickly faded into fall; not long after, we got our first dose of nor'easters and bone-chilling winters – a far cry from our sub-tropical climate in South Carolina. During our first winter there I learned how to shovel snow, salt the walkways, and actually saw the mercury drop to zero on the thermometer.

As winter seized the Northeast, fear and anxiety began to invade my heart. Everything was cold, and people seemed to grow colder. The new church folks were warm and gracious enough, but in my high school with 3,000 plus students, I was just a stocky Southern kid in the twilight zone of puberty. In this strange world of Yankee accents and gigantic buildings, I felt my fledgling identity begin to shrink. Many nights found me crying to sleep, wondering how I would survive in a place that did not speak the familiar language of *hey ya'll*. I felt so alone, misplaced and a bit abandoned.

The kids in the neighborhood were little help. At times, they were downright cruel. One morning, during the twenty-minute wait at the bus stop, my peers took their regular target practice at my southern accent. They threw darts at my culture and my gross lack of "urban savvy."

In one incident that remains vivid in my memory, my ignorance shined like a full harvest moon! One of the guys—in jest—and unbeknownst to me, wisecracked about how "GQ" my clothes looked. This term never surfaced in my southern past. I had no idea what GQ meant. Maybe it meant "cool," and indicated that I was moving closer to acceptance.

All of the guys awaited my response. 'Dewayne' asked, "Hey Potter, what does GQ mean?" Gulp, hard question with no good answer. So I popped out with the first thing that came to mind. *"Good quality?"* Ouch. My answer sealed my stupidity in their minds and became ammunition for numerous other pot shots at my intellect. I can laugh about it all now, but back then, I felt like a Southern misfit. Their rejection magnified my craving to belong.

Thankfully, God used my stocky build and athletic ability and over time through football and lacrosse, I finally did gain acceptance in high school. Unfortunately, I soon found out that sex, drugs, and rebellion played on those teams as well.

I realize now that the abundance of new experiences both good and bad, are tools that God ultimately uses to craft his will in us and expand our spiritual horizons. He allows our spiritual skin to thicken for his purposes. God knew that one day the fish-out-of-water Southern kid would preach the Gospel in some tough spots, including the largest Muslim country in the world - where a past of rejection can come in pretty handy I might add.

In the upheaval of those years God never left me. I had several spiritual epiphanies and at age eighteen, I felt the call on my life to full-time ministry. But the *glass house* was far too fragile a place to live permanently, or so I thought. I had zero desire back then to follow in my dad's footsteps,

I began a marathon to distance myself from anything that would ever look like the pulpit. I knew one thing for sure; I'd never pursue anything that remotely resembled the ministry. But as Lisa, my wife often says, "God is the last comic standing!"

I survived high school, made it through college and eventually graduate school. By the grace of God, my college sweetheart became my wife, and Lisa and I started our pursuit of the American Dream. I *almost* reached it. Soon, I had a six-figure income to share with my beautiful partner. I was enjoying corporate jet privileges, a great house in the right neighborhood, and we had three amazing children. I was living what vaguely resembled the alluring credit card commercial opening with the bit about priceless moments: *There are some things money can't buy.....for everything else there is MasterCard®...*

Yes, I had arrived at last and reached a pinnacle of success. Sadly, it describes a way of living, but it was far from being *priceless,* at least for me. Benjamin Franklin said there are no gains without pains, and many of us find that after pursuing our material dreams, the cost is heavy and the burden colossal. Every day greeted *me* with the anxiety that I could lose it all at any given moment. Even more, deep inside this outwardly prosperous man hid a broken little boy.

At the height of my corporate career, I found myself on the flip side of where I should be. I lived a life crawling in contradictions. On the outside I stood as a man of integrity, who advertised Joshua 24:15 *"As for me and my household, we will serve the Lord."* On the inside stooped a man of countless secret compromises. The disparity began to erode my soul. I can personally attest to what Graham Green, a prolific English novelist, wrote: "Success is more dangerous than failure. The ripples break over a wider coastline."[2]

Psychologists have a term they use called cognitive dissonance.

Wikipedia describes it this way: *Cognitive dissonance –* "the term to define the condition that results whenever an individual attempts to hold two incompatible, if not contradictory thoughts at the same time, even in the face of mounting evidence to the contrary."

In retrospect, I realize now that not only were my thoughts dissonant, *my life was dissonant.*

This dissonance is very similar to what the Apostle James calls "double mindedness." (James 1:8) James is referring to those who waffle in conviction, and says that the result of this condition is an unstable character, like huge waves, constantly rolling, pushed and pulled by wind and tide, tossed about randomly. Such people are inconsistent, insecure, dizzy—unstable.

This description nailed who I was. In addition, I was convinced that my success had to have been a fluke. My charm and wit must have promoted my climb up the corporate latter. And my spiritual charade—that fine cloak of integrity I wore so well—gave no hint of the morally and sexually broken man who mocked me in the mirror each morning. If *they* only knew the real me, it would soon all be over. Sadly, these thoughts just didn't creep up and pounce on me one day. They had been my constant companions since I understood how to think about thinking.

Well, yes I had arrived, but where and when was the big reward? At what point was I scheduled to receive my *man badge*? I looked like a man, talked like a man, and posed for family portraits like a man; but at the end of the day, fulfillment eluded me like Leonardo Di Caprio who evaded Tom Hanks in the movie, *Catch me if You Can*. I felt like Solomon writing of the human dilemma at the end of his life. Ecclesiastes is full of warnings and predictions about the mirages of life that lead to emptiness and despair.

Every rung on my ladder of success was notched with a failed attempt for affirmation. Vanity, vanity, just as King Solomon writes in Ecclesiastes 1:2. He concludes from this dissection of life, that all pursuits under the sun are meaningless, and in the end what matters is that we fear God and keep his commandments. *This is the duty of man*. (Eccl. 12:13). His words pave the way for the realization that true contentment can only be found in Christ.

As you might guess, I never acquired my "man badge." The *system*, the world and all its pursuits, couldn't produce what my spirit craved most—deep and reciprocal intimacy with Father God.

Yes, I knew wrong and I knew right, but it didn't prevent me from plunging into sin. I had no clue how to joyfully live out the faith I'd been raised in. My life spiraled into spiritual schizophrenia. I did not know who I was, nor did I know how to find me. At thirty-two, I found myself broken, empty, angry, and frustrated, believing the Church had failed me—or I had failed the Church. And as for the call on my life to preach that I sensed when I was eighteen, it had to have been ruined by my past and mirage of character. If I did somehow make Heaven, I would have to spend eternity in remorse for abandoning that voice that wooed me years earlier. There must be penance to pay for so much lost time.

I loathed who I had become and cried out to God to change me...change me into whatever he wanted, change my perception of who he was...but somehow please *change me*. These words of Jesus now resonate so true to me: "If you remain in me and my words remain in you," Jesus said, "ask whatever you wish, and it will be given to you." (John 15:7 NIV)

Truth, give me truth. That's what I longed for. When we know the truth, the truth sets us free. When the Greek philosopher, Socrates, found himself convicted of undermining state religion and corrupting young people, he addressed the jury telling them he refused to abandon his pursuit of the truth. Public discussion of the great issues of life and virtue are a necessary part of any valuable human life, he said, and *"the unexamined life is not worth living,"* Socrates was saying he would rather die than give up his search for truth. I wanted truth as a drowning man wants air. Ending the charade, coming out from behind the façade meant coming clean with my secret sins, losing my good reputation in the church, and with my own kids.

At this point in my life I was about to witness Jesus' words ring painfully true:

There is nothing hidden that will not be revealed, nothing secret that will not become known and come to the light.

(Luke 8:17)

Chapter 2

Exposing the Orphan Spirit

...There, they shall be called sons of the living God.

(Romans 9:26)

A s with every great testimony of healing, mine begins with great pain. As C.S. Lewis said about pain, it's God's megaphone to rouse a deaf world. [3]

Before I expound on more of my story, I want to share what I believe to be the foundational lie upon which Satan erects every other stronghold. Perhaps like me, you might have swallowed this deception and experienced the subsequent brokenness it brings. It took me forty years to discover what you are about to read in this chapter. Hopefully, you'll be a much quicker study.

In several passages of scripture, angels are given the title of the *sons* of God. (Genesis 6:2-4, Job 1:6 through 2:1, then again in 38:7). Let me first clarify here, that Lucifer and the other angels *were in no way "sons of God" in the class of Jesus, the second person of the Godhead.* Jesus is the only begotten of the Father and the only one ever qualified to sit on the throne at the Father's right hand. *Nevertheless*, the angels were given this title in portions of scripture and enjoyed at least some measure of fellowship with our Father on the lines of sons.

However, in Luke 10:18, Jesus tells us that in a millisecond, Lucifer was irrevocably evicted from Heaven and cut off from his privileged state,... *"I saw Satan fall like lightening from Heaven."* The book of Revelation indicates a third of Heaven's angelic host fell with Lucifer as well. I believe with this fall, that Lucifer, the light bearer, may have experienced the most painful metamorphosis ever recorded.

In a flash he changed from Lucifer - a prince of angels, to Satan - the original orphan spirit.

We think of an orphan as one who has been deprived of their parents somehow. This was not the case with Lucifer. Through pride and rebellion, his relationship with his Father was forever forfeited, and his future eternally damned. We now know that this event set the stage for him to become the adversary of God, his children, and all that would ever be good.

Travel with me to a place called eternity past, to an event before time existed. I want you to imagine what *might* have crossed Lucifer's mind in the aftermath of "The Fall." Suddenly, the crowning star of Heaven's angelic host is cut off from a fellowship that existed through eons of time. His status as an archangel is lost. His rebellion cost him and countless other cherubim eternal banishment from God's goodness. He would never again walk as a citizen of love, light, joy, bliss, peace, fellowship, and every other perfect gift.

This one act of selfishness struck an eternal discord to the harmony of existence. Now not only was Heaven altered, but the entire universe tilted on its axis as evil defined.

Eternity, that had never known anything but *us*, now must recognize *them*.

Division was the first byproduct of the fall. Before this event there was only perfect unity in Heaven. Since then, everything that flows from Satan is discordant in nature. He assumed that through division he could weaken God. Obviously he was wrong; however, separation and then isolation are still part of his primary strategies against us.

As Lucifer and his cohorts are cast from Heaven to earth, they experience changes far beyond our comprehension; however, none as somber as this: Satan though not alone, would now be forever *lonely*.

An interesting fact: the word *orphan* in the Bible doesn't necessarily refer to being without parents, but can be used figuratively for one who is without a teacher and a guide. When we have no spiritual guardian, we wander aimlessly and alone. The Hebrew word for orphan is yäthōm, which actually means *lonely*.

From the time of his fall from grace, the devil has sought to multiply the pain of his orphan heart to all who will listen. His only voice is the sinister whisper of deceit. He slithers on the scene when we are wounded and/or vulnerable. He softly sows seeds of doubt and distrust, twisting what we know from God's word to be true. Jesus told us in John 8:44 that Satan is the father of lies and incapable of speaking the truth, yet he speaks. His modus operandi is simple but lethal.

From his first appearance in Eden, Satan has sought to cause God's children to question their Father's love.

Notice in the Garden of Eden, Satan did not question Eve regarding God's existence, or even if He cared or loved her. Satan tempted Eve with the thought that God did not love her <u>enough</u>. Eve is the first being on earth to be emotionally attacked by Satan, spiritually mugged if you will.

Satan succeeded in painting the path for her decline. She succumbed to his deceit, to his appealing hints that *God is unfair* and that he withholds his best from us. A tactic he still uses very skillfully today. He manipulated Eve's trust in God by sowing the *if only* seed. *"If only you eat the fruit...you will be like God."* How often do we give way to enticements like this today?

He used a similar tactic in the story surrounding Jesus' temptation in the wilderness. The end of Matthew chapter three gives us the account of Jesus' baptism. What an awesome event in the history of the world. Humanity gets the rare opportunity to see the Godhead manifest. The Son rises out of the water glistening from his baptism by John. The Holy Spirit lights upon Jesus in the form of a dove. Then, the culmination of honor comes as the booming voice of the Father declares, *"This is my beloved Son in whom I am well pleased!"*

With this proclamation, I imagine that all of Heaven roared in applause as God the Father finally gets to shout a thirty-year belated birth announcement. *This is my boy, and I absolutely love everything about him!*

Now, cut to the scene of a barren, dry and lonely place. Immediately after this fantastic display of the Trinity, inexplicably, the Holy Spirit lunges Jesus into a place and season called the wilderness. We know of nothing Jesus had done to merit banishment to this place. In fact, scripture later reveals that he always did what pleased his Father.

Yet, Jesus, who just received the highest honor from the highest voice, is suddenly alone and seemingly un-honored and unarmed.

Satan is waiting. He studies the Son of God for forty days and nights as the fast takes it toil. *Finally,* Jesus is weak, hungry, and vulnerable. Satan strikes. He recalls and mocks the words that the Father had spoken not too many days earlier…"*My beloved Son.*" It is in this context, in Matthew 4:3, that we hear the original orphan's first words to Jesus. "*If you are the son of God…*"

Of the infinite things that Satan could have said at this reunion, he asked this question, and then "dared" Jesus to turn stones to bread. What prompted Satan to ask this question? My first response would be to remember what Jesus told us in Matthew 4:15, "*When the word of God goes forth, immedi-*

ately Satan comes to steal it." Not too many days earlier at the Jordan River, God had declared Jesus' sonship at his baptism. Obviously, Satan desired to refute God's word.

However, I believe there was likely something much more insidious and profound going on than meets the eye in this dialogue. Perhaps this question flowed out of the deepest pain in Satan's heart. I wonder if he could not endure the agony of knowing that Jesus, *now on his turf*, was still enjoying perfect sonship with Abba Father.

Consider this. The only two citizens of earth who had tasted the joy of intimate communion with the Father in Heaven were Satan and Jesus. While there were a myriad of other fallen angels, none of them had access to God as *he* once did. I imagine that it was then and there, face to face with Jesus, that the memories of a billion yesterdays began to flood Satan's mind, when *Lucifer* enjoyed a measure of sonship with God.

This parched and barren wilderness was an accurate depiction of Satan's existence since his fall from Heaven. He was lifeless, hopeless and eternally thirsty for the fellowship that he once knew.

Satan now must face what *Lucifer* had forfeited so very long ago. Jesus still had fellowship. Jesus was still God's beloved.

Satan was not. I believe the jealousy that fueled his original fall now again cried out the most painful "if" ever to be spoken.

I often wonder if Satan loathes this little word above all others. This tiny preposition is one of the most empowering and impregnating words in linguistics; in fact, it has initiated every salvation that has ever occurred…"*If we confess our sins, He is faithful and just to forgive us…*" (1 John 1:9). However, for Satan, it is the most damning….*if* he had dealt with his pride, *if* he had not rebelled, if he would have changed his course of action. This tiny word reminds him of what he lost, now hopelessly irrecoverable.

The great news for us is that God obviously had a grand plan in Jesus' temptation. Through their dialogue in the wilderness, our Father allows us to observe Satan's chief strategy against the believer and the Church:

Satan questioned Jesus' identity. His first assault was to make Jesus feel *illegitimate*.

This is exactly what he incessantly tries to do to us. His chief offensive is to rob of us of our identity in Christ and convince us we are abandoned, alone, and misunderstood. He wants us to experience the totality of his existence, *orphaned and hopeless*.

In his Divine Comedy, the entrance into Dante's Inferno has these words inscribed, "Abandon hope all ye who enter here." There is no more desolate place than that place of hopelessness. Satan knows that God's sons and daughters, even when we stumble and fall from his plan, still have the hope of renewed fellowship. He does not and never will.

I know this kind of illegitimacy and the pain and fear it spawns. It has been thirty plus years, and I am still on my journey of complete healing from an orphan heart. I was eight years old when the brokenness began.

He, (who remains nameless), was in his late teens, and kept me in his room to watch over me as my parents had lunch with his one Sunday after church. His father was a deacon and his mother was active in women's ministry. These good Christian people had no clue at the time, that their son whom they trusted to babysit me, was struggling with homosexuality, would one day be immersed in the gay culture, and eventually die from AIDS.

When "it" happened, I knew something awful had transpired, but words would not come, only a silent scream. If you or someone you know has been through a similar experience, then you are familiar with the terror, the anger, the shame of it.

When we are violated in such a way, we panic at the thought of coming clean, telling the truth, for fear of being blamed. Oddly, my first thoughts were of getting in trouble. Remember, I was raised in a family line of staunch fire-breathing Pentecostals, *with a zero tolerance for impurity I might add*. A bad thing just happened, an awful thing.

Telling my parents might make it worse. Then I thought of him, the sitter, the older kid I once admired. Maybe he didn't really mean it. And what might they do to him? Like many abuse victims, I cleverly masked the pain that ultimately would fester into a lifelong struggle of sexual brokenness.

Looking back, my innocence wasn't the only thing violated that momentous day; it was the unspoken promise of protection from my parents as well. Naturally, they knew nothing of what happened, and they'd never have put me in that position had they been at all suspicious. And once they did find out, they would have intervened, but it would have opened the proverbial can of worms...worms without end, so my young mind thought.

The deceiver knew how it would all play out. He enjoyed the whole scenario, from planting the perverted thoughts in a young man's head, to watching him carry it out on me. The Bible says it all: *The thief comes only to steal and kill and destroy,* (John 10:10). In that vulnerable and devastating moment, *evil* whispered to my tender heart the lie I believed for so long, *if God really loved you Jon, why did he allow this to happen?*

We've all had these thoughts when troubles come our way, disasters we don't understand, and we wonder if our pain might be too insignificant to a God who has watching over the whole world on his "to do" list?

My thoughts went something like this: *If I just ignore it all, it will all go away.* Not hardly. Satan knows our human nature, our natural response. If he could somehow convince my young impressionable mind that God did not love me, by using the wilderness tactic he used on Jesus, ("*If you are the son of God*"), then he could steal what the Father had planned for my life.

The devil was out to destroy my destiny and his scheme nearly worked. The molestation opened my innocent and trusting heart to fear. Worse, it enticed my soul to carnal knowledge. That one "if" pierced my wounded soul and laid the foundation of thousands of broken thoughts and behaviors.

Satan did not have to work overtime to convince me that God—who didn't protect me, who allowed this travesty—was untrustworthy. How could I ever believe he would take care of me, that he loved me...like Eve in the garden, that he loved me *enough?*

A passion for self preservation and self defense kicked in. If you've seen the movie *Karate Kid* from 1984, you remember newcomer Daniel, (played by Ralph Macchio), getting beat up by local bullies, all adept in karate. Determined to stick up for himself, Daniel starts to teach himself martial arts. Everything in him says to fight back, get tough so *you won't get hurt again.* An accurate picture of me after my experience.

For Christmas that same year, I remember asking Santa for a weight set, telling my dad, "I'm gonna be huge one day." He chuckled and gave me the thumbs up. Looking back, I think my parents considered their son an overzealous comic book fan, sketching out my heroes on any blank piece of paper and daydreaming of saving the world. Little did they know of my inner vow; *never again will I get caught in a weak or vulnerable position to anyone.*

Strength became my everything. Schwarzenegger the Terminator became my idol. *I'll be back.*

While aspiring for brawn and power, I had no inkling just how vulnerable the molestation had made me. It had prematurely opened a door in my soul to a visitor bent on my destruction. Satan was waiting to strike at me, again and again. Shortly after the incident, pornography came my way, and that *virus* almost destroyed me. I now call it the AIDS of the soul.

Buffing up my body and building muscle might help me fend off a future pedophile, but there were no weapons in my arsenal for what would turn into a thirty-year war against the spirit of perversion.

It happened one day while I was playing hide and seek with two of my childhood friends, just down the road from my house in the field behind the local middle school. I ran to escape the countdown: *"Five, four, three, two, one…ready or not, here I come…"* To avoid discovery, I dove into a ditch behind the playground. I was found all right, but not by my friends. As I looked around to get my bearings after I jumped in the ditch, I found myself staring at three extremely lewd and graphic magazines, discarded by some other captive soul.

My pre-teen curiosity took the bait of the enemy, and from that point on, pornography became my invisible attraction and my silent sin. It remained with me throughout my teenage years and matured into my master in adulthood. It was such a part of my life, that I planned my schedule around it. Not only was I hooked, but it drove me to being promiscuous with any willing girl, any time, any place, thus fulfilling the words of Solomon in Proverbs 23:7, "As a man thinks in his heart so is he."

Watchman Nee said, *what you behold, you will eventually become.*

I became someone, someone I despised. Sensual pleasures left me hollow, calloused and unable to receive any kind of real love. All the girls who believed my lies—and later all the women—became conquests. Promiscuity, and then drug abuse to numb the pain of my sin, were my teenage rites of passage into manhood.

This story is all too real and poignant for me, and I'm sure for many others.

In the last thirty years I've listened to countless stories of men and women who've known the same brokenness. Whether from abuse or abandonment, it is the same sense of loss and betrayal.

Left unhealed, the pain drives you to behaviors you never imagined you would consider; much less, engage in. This cycle of bondage is irrespective of gender, race, pedigree, education or religious affiliation. Countless men, and now more and more women, find themselves statistics to pornography's tyranny and aftermath of destruction.

The stories are almost identical: Exposure, curiosity, fascination, indulgence, addiction...*death*. James 1:15 tells us that when sin is conceived it brings forth death.

Every person who has experienced this cycle has "died" to something precious along the way.

For me, it became a death to normal sexual development and appropriate relationships with my peers. It brought on the end of my innocence and childhood frivolity. Complete freedom to simply be and enjoy spontaneous laughter and silliness, which should have been the hallmarks of my childhood, were always overshadowed by a dark specter of the "if then" from that Sunday afternoon. These simple joys went missing like a lost child on a milk carton, never to be recovered. Even with my best intentions; ultimately, every relational attempt with a member of the opposite sex was sabotaged by a covert agenda for promiscuity. Just as James predicted, parts of me were bound up and dead like Lazarus of old, and oh how desperately I needed a resurrection and life!

This is not the place to explore the colossal issue of sexual brokenness, but let me say that it is only defeated through the delivering work of Calvary, grace, and consistent accountability. We will explore these in greater depths in chapters 8 and 9.

Now, in this healing season of my life, I boast triumphantly that God is doing as he promised—restoring all that I lost. And regardless of where *you've* been wounded, he's promised to do the same, to make up for what has been stolen from *you*. I've come to realize that

He really can give you beauty for ashes—*even if you started the fire yourself.*

Restoration is the work our Father majors in!

Satan, the accuser, the deceiver, sought to violate something much more eternal than my body; *he wanted me to believe I was abandoned and illegitimate*. Maybe Satan has planted that same *"if...then"* seed in you. Your story may be much more horrific or maybe more benign. Either way, he wants you to believe that you are orphaned, a stray who is unauthorized for entry into God's family, unqualified to be loved and used for his glory.

We first learn about fatherhood from our own fathers. You may have grown up with an absentee father; either physically or emotionally distant. Men struggle with learning to be the Father's son.

For women deprived of a daddy's love, it's normal to harbor a distrust of men and struggle to embrace the reality of being a daughter of God. Whatever our story, if we allow Satan's seeds of doubt to take root and mature, they cause us to reap a life far below the regal position for which we are born.

I think of Esther, born for "such a time as this."

When we meet her in Esther chapter two, we learn she is a Jewish orphan, adopted and raised her by her cousin Mordecai. When Persian King Zerxes decides to banish Queen Vashti, he orders a search of beautiful girls throughout the land to find her replacement. This young woman is snatched from all she knows and trusts and forced to enter a beauty contest for one night with a heathen king. Despite the outcome, she will never return to her old life. The Bible does not reveal any doubts she might have had about God's faithfulness, and there must have been many, but Esther the orphan becomes the confident queen who knows who she is meant to be. Only a heart that understands Romans 8:31 can risk losing it all. *"If God is for us, who can be against us?"* We know that Esther's courage saved the entire Jewish nation.

Some of us still respond and react as though we are orphans, simply existing, stuck in holding patterns, clueless how to experience the warmth of the Father's heart that infuses us with the courage to do his will.

There is no shame in needing to be re-parented. All of us at some point in life need it, and God will craft and implement a unique plan, tailor made for our needs, gifts and personality. He is the expert on bringing up his kids. It comforts me to know what St. Augustine said is true. "God loves each of us as if there were only one of us," regardless of the wounds we have endured.

Chapter Three

Healing The Orphan Spirit

I will not leave you *orphans*; I will come to you.

(John 14:15-18)

The orphan heart never feels it has a permanent safe and secure place where it can be loved, valued and affirmed. *The orphan heart is often frozen in yesterday's pain.*

Yesterday's pain can cycle through your mind and paralyze your thoughts like a perpetual ice cream brain freeze. Invariably, a mental and emotional freeze often occurred with me just as I was about to step into a birthright of blessing as God's child. I would be making progress in my walk with God; then unexpectedly, some painful event would occur, or a loved one would face a crisis, and I'd boomerang back into orphan thinking and illegitimacy. Satan would rev up again, spinning those "*if*" and "*then*" messages at me - confirming my feelings of abandonment. My faith walk would stall and often halt altogether.

In counseling others, I've yet to find an orphan heart who is not incapacitated in life by something, most often it is fear. *The orphan heart is plagued by fear.* Fear of lack. Fear of failure. Fear of sickness. We with orphan hearts are petrified of dying. The abandoned heart fears the stress of today and the skeletons of yesterday. It exists as a life full of extremes, desiring to be crucified with Christ, yet being unable to let go of the law of self-preservation.

It is a heart way overdrawn in so many of the accounts of life. It *dreams* about living a life that is exceedingly, abundantly above all it can ask, but *lives in* the world of barely getting by through the sweat of its brow. Masked in a veneer of humor, my true heart became cynical and rarely accepted love at face value. The end-result for those like me is a calcification of emotions and ultimately, a heart full of knotted bitter roots.

Orphaned hearts see the successes of others, but either criticizes them or stews in envy.

This heart can never fully rejoice with others because it lost its joy somewhere along the way. It dwells outside of the goodness of God, outside the land of those fully alive in Christ, ever taunted by the *orphaned accuser of the brethren*. How do I know? Because I lived this way for so long…broken heartbeat after broken heartbeat. My pain was too heavy to own and even more difficult to admit to the world. Possibly, you have seen a glimpse of yourself in these descriptions and wonder is there any way out.

Well my friend, if any of what I have described resonates with your experience, I have genuine and wonderful news for you! Jesus promises the glorious coming of the Holy Spirit to all who have ever felt illegitimate or abandoned! Let me remind you again of his wonderful promise in John 14:18, *I will not leave you orphans; I will come to you.*

Some modern translations substitute the word "comfortless" here for orphans, however, in the Greek, the word Jesus used was simply *orphanos*, which means fatherless or parentless. I assure you his word choice was not accidental.

The context of Jesus' statement is right before his ascension, where he will no longer physically be with his disciples. Remember, he has been with them nearly every day for three years. At this point, Jesus has become their rabbi, their confidante, and very best friend. He is now their messiah and God.

Jesus knew Satan's plan. The deceiver would enact the same strategy of the wilderness, the same strategy he used in Eden. Despite being with him continuously for three years, Jesus understood that the disciples were still susceptible to the fear and brokenness caused by abandonment. He vows to them in assurance, "I will not leave you orphans..." Healing for the orphan heart begins by embracing this truth and grasping the revelation from the two verses *prior* to this one:

"If you love Me, keep My commandments. And I will pray the *Father*, and He will give you another Helper, that He may *abide with you forever*, the Spirit of truth whom the world cannot receive because it neither sees Him nor knows Him; but you know Him, for He dwells with you and will be in you. 18 I will not leave you *orphans*; I will come to you."

(John 14:15-18)

Jesus stresses that The Holy Spirit will not just abide with us temporarily, but that he is forever with us having one objective: He is our constant help. While The Spirit is down here with us on earth, Jesus has assumed the posture as our Divine Intercessor, ever praying for you and me!

Working together, Jesus and The Holy Spirit ensure that the Father's will manifests here on earth as it is done in Heaven. Imagine that, The Spirit and Son operating in perfect agreement as mentioned in Matthew 18:19. Friend, Jesus instituted the prayer of agreement on earth and now through The Holy Spirit - enforces its power from Heaven!

The great news as I mentioned earlier is that Jesus' prayer has never ceased. He is still covering every one of God's children in prayer today, right now, this second! He is interceding that you will come into the fullness of the truth that God loves you and will never abandon you. Regarding prayer, consider this: Jesus walked with humanity for thirty years. He ministered to humanity for three years; however, since his ascension, *Jesus has been praying for humanity for over two thousand years!*

He vows to abide in you with his Holy Spirit GPS, which will navigate you through the pain of life and unmask the deceit of the evil one. I remember when I used my first GPS unit, and when missing the exit, she (such a pleasant voice), would always say, "Recalculating route, recalculating…"

The Holy Spirit is the guiding power of God. Whenever you have decisions to make or when you've made the wrong turn, he is there to guide you, to show you the best way on the road you find yourself on. He's always recalculating when we miss life's turns. He points us in one direction, back home to our Father.

The Holy Spirit, our Comforter, is also ever present, ever working and knows your exact life-coordinates. If we are wounded along the way, he comes along as the best physician there is to minister his healing grace and tender mercy. He will not leave us in the hour of our greatest wounding.

Because he knew that one day we would all be left for dead by some unjustness on our respective roads in life, Jesus gave us the story of the Good Samaritan.

The principles of the Samaritan's story are still vividly true today. Jesus is still our peace and picks us up off the road of our brokenness. He has purchased a room of salvation for us to stay in, all the while funding our provision while we heal. He commits us to the care of The Holy Spirit, who is the innkeeper of our lives, who nurses us back to health until The Master returns for his people. Halleluiah!

You and I also need to know that The Holy Spirit refuses to allow you to feel stupid in life's challenges. He has graduated *summa cum laude* of every subject that has ever been at any time or any place; furthermore, he is delighted to constantly be with you whenever you need a tutor and friend.

What am I saying to you? I hope you will comprehend that in a world that values the strong surviving, and only gives performance-based acceptance, his Holy Spirit will forever be all the affirmation you need!

He will not leave us as orphans, he will come to us.

What do you need him to be for you right now? What walls of adversity are standing between you and wholeness, between you and your destiny? Jesus Christ, The Lord of Heaven's host, is ready to march around these walls with an angelic army and shout for them to crumble!

The book of Hebrews tells us that Christ lives to intercede for you. He is calling you to shake off the shackles of ten thousand failures and every weight that so easily hinders you. (Hebrews 12: 1). You have God's DNA running through every particle of your spirit, and our savior so wants you to experience the fullness of your inheritance. You too are a BELOVED child of God!

There, they shall be called sons of the living God.

(Romans 9:26)

I encourage you to remember when Satan whispered and you believed. Was there a moment or series of events that told you God was not real and if he was, you surely were not worthy of his love? The truth is that none of us are worthy, but there is one who was and is and who is able to far-exceed all you can ask or think - Jesus Christ the Righteous!

Child of Royalty, believe this. Jesus accepts you, so his Father accepts you. He embraces you, so the Father embraces you. He delights in you, so the Father delights in you. His love beckons you from the vacuum of orphan existence into the birthright He purchased with his own blood.

Jesus said in Matthew 11:27 that no one can know Father God unless he reveals the Father to them. Did you know that this was (and still is) one of Jesus' primary objectives? He really wants you and me to know our Daddy. Oh, what manner of love the Father has lavished on us that we could become his children. Hear and believe the words of the Apostle Paul once more:

For you are all sons of God through faith in Christ Jesus. (Galatians 3:26)

Your faith and my faith has given us what Satan will never possess. We are God's children by faith and through love. If you are uncertain of a love that will not abandon you, I encourage you to open your heart and turn to the next chapter. You just might receive a new revelation about who our Father really is, and just how far his amazing love extends.

Chapter 4

Who's Your Abba

*All things have been delivered to Me by My Father,
and no one knows the Son except the Father. Nor does
anyone know the Father except the Son, and the one to
whom the Son wills to reveal Him.*

(Matthew 11:27-28)

He has many names in our culture - *Father, Daddy, Pop, Dad,* and for some, even *My Old Man.* His name means something different to every one of us. Unfortunately, to multitudes, *he* does not exist at all. For them, the only proof that fatherhood ever occurred is a birth certificate tucked away in some cabinet or drawer full of sundries. To them, that name is nothing more than a lifeless noun. Whatever that word means to any of us, even the very best example we could produce is a fractured and pale expression of who Jesus introduces in Matthew Chapter 6, verse 9, "Our *Father…*"

This introduction by Jesus was the beginning of the end to a long-held perception that God was mystical, aloof, angry, and even violent. In addition, to the Jews, the God of the Old Testament was certainly unapproachable by unholy mere men. However, Jesus, who Hebrews Chapter 1 declares is the carbon copy of the Father, introduced a revolution of how to know God, believe in God, observe God, but most of all, *love God and be loved by Him!*

Ponder this. Until Jesus was introduced to us in Matthew, God the Father had all of eternity past and eternity future to reveal who he was to humanity. He decides to re-present himself, and compresses this revelation into the three-year window of Jesus' ministry. He sends Jesus as his high definition replica and Heaven's ambassador.

Sending Jesus, God declares to the world, if you really want to know what *I am like,* then watch how my Son spends his free time:

I like hang to out with the *unpopular,* the *broken,* the *misfits,* the *hated,* the *lonely,* and yes, *children.* I am a listener, a healer, a restorer, and your friend; by the way, you are officially invited to be my child forever!

You may be like me, and due to your past experience, have a limited, distorted, or completely obscured view of *this* kind of God. To you the name father may be synonymous with words that are very uncomfortable: words like absent, indifferent, inconsistent, rejection, anger, abuse, or possibly even abandonment.

Undoubtedly, the imprint that parents make on our lives is indelible. Though often unintended, that imprint is sometimes indelibly painful. Often it remains as a painful *tattoo* upon our souls, regardless of the plateaus we achieve in life.

In James Dobson's book, *Bringing Up Boys*, he tells a story about former first lady Hillary Rodham Clinton, whose father never affirmed her as a child. When she was in high school, she brought home a straight-A report card, showed it to him, hoping for a word of commendation. Instead he uttered, "Well, you must be attending an easy school." Thirty-five years later, the remark still burns in Mrs. Clinton's mind."[4]

Our childhood pain and experiences strongly influence our perception of Father God and the way we relate or fail to relate to Him in our world. *This perception affects our adult response to his love.* Aldous Huxley once said, "There are things known and there are things unknown, and in between are the doors of perception."[5]

Perception then is the sum of our experiences good or bad, which comprise the optic through which we view life. In addition to our orphan thinking, many of us are unable to receive Abba Father's love due to parental wounding that has not healed. Simply, our *optic* is cracked, and we have an incomplete understanding of the reality and magnitude of God's love. Truth be known, our parents most likely experienced love through this same cracked generational optic and often gave us the best they could.

Thomas Kempis, a medieval monk who wrote The Imitation of Christ, once said, "If we knew all, we could pardon all." This is so true, as often we only really see the tip of each other's persona iceberg, and certainly don't know the depths of pain that our fellow man carries.

My author friend, Jan Coleman, writes about this in her book *Woman Behind the Mask*. Raised in a troubled home, she kept her distance from her mother whose drinking bouts always brought on verbal abuse.

Her mother's alcoholism caused this only child to erect a wall of protection and don the clown mask. "Humor was my secret weapon against all the hurt," she says. Jan married young and hasty, and spent years trying to keep up the façade of the perfect family. When her husband abandoned the family, all Jan's masks fell away. "And it was painful. Some of my masks were attached with super glue," she adds.

As she says, *we change when the pain of staying the same is worse than the pain of changing.* "Like you, Jon, I asked God to change me, no matter what it took. Make me into your woman. Grow me into someone like yourself." She went into a year of intense Christian counseling where she began to heal and forgive those who hurt her.

After Jan's father died, her mother fell apart and eventually fell in to the arms of Jesus. One day she said, "I'm sorry—for the way I treated you all those years," and told Jan her back-story. Alice lost her father at a very vulnerable age, and then worked to help support her widowed mother. She fell in love with a wealthy boy from the city. 'I wasn't good enough for his family," she said, and choked on the next few words. "I got... pregnant and his family told him if he married me they would disinherit him. They paid for...the abortion."

Suddenly all the pieces of the puzzle fell into place, the lost clues to her mother's alcoholism. The good Catholic girl from New England had swept her shame under the rug, buried her past, but could never fully love or bond with her only child. [6]

One secret shame tarnished the woman Alice was meant to be. Finally understanding her mother's back-story, what happened to her long ago, helped Jan to see why she responded to life the way she did, and this truth was a healing truth.

The sad truth is that since the fall of Adam and Eve, broken parents have loved in broken ways, and children have experienced the *fallout*. Many of us have naturally assumed that the way our parents loved us is how our Heavenly Father loves us.

However, any perception of your Heavenly Father other than one of agape love, is inaccurate.

If you are unfamiliar with agape, you need to know it is the kind of love that is mentioned most often in the New Testament. It is the only cure for the wounded soul and orphaned heart. In order for us to better understand its meaning, we will quickly examine what it is *not*.

The ancient Greeks had four primary words to communicate love: eros, phileo, stergo, and agape.

- *Eros* can be described as a lower a form of physical love. It is probably more akin to lust, physical desire and sexual release than it is love.

- *Phileo* is a more noble emotion than eros. This love depicts *affection* between couples; it can be explained as the camaraderie between friends and is often called brotherly love.

- *Stergo* raises the bar even higher. It can be defined as that love that exists between members of a family. This love is a committed love. Stergo can be described as unflinching fidelity between parties to stay together when the going gets tough.

All of these have their place; however, if *agape* is the Father's kind of love, then surely it merits deeper exploration.

In his book, *Sparkling Gems from the Greek*, Rick Renner describes agape as, "high-level love, for there is no higher, finer, or more excellent love than agape love." He further writes, "Agape is so filled with deep emotion and meaning, that it is one of the most difficult words to translate in the New Testament.

Agape occurs when and individual sees, recognizes, understands or appreciates the value of an object or a person, causing the viewer to behold this object or person in great esteem, awe, admiration, wonder and sincere appreciation. Great respect awakes in the heart of the observer for the object or person he is beholding, that he is compelled to love it. In fact, his love for that person or object is so strong that it is irresistible."[7]

You and I in all our brokenness, with all our character flaws, inconsistencies and failures, are still irresistible to our Heavenly Father! The best part—agape is drawn to brokenness, it exists for brokenness.

Steve Franklin, whose ministry I joined when I left corporate America, is one of my first spiritual fathers beyond my childhood. One day we were chatting about what God's love really looks like, and Steve gave me the best revelation of this God-kind of love that I have ever heard:

> **Agape is *unconditional*:** There is absolutely nothing we could ever do or fail to do to receive it.
>
> **Agape is *undiminished*.** His love will never fade in its intensity. Like the noonday sun in a cloudless sky, it beams as bright in our *failures* as it does is in our *successes*.
>
> **Agape is *unrelenting*:** It is like the waves of the ocean that incessantly pound against the shore. It will tirelessly pursue us until we receive its embrace!

Wow, who would not want to receive this kind of amazing love? *Agape!*

The question begs to be asked. How did the church lose sight of this revelation of what our Father's love really looks like? Through Jesus' example, John the Beloved certainly understood Abba's love. He says in 1 John 4:16 that *"God is love*, and he who abides in love abides in God and God in him."* Of course, the word that John refers to here is agape.

I urge you to meditate on 1 Corinthians Chapter 13. No wonder these verses have been recited at nearly every Christian wedding ceremony that has ever been. But the greater message the Holy Spirit was writing to the Corinthian Church—and to us—is that that our Dad wanted to undeniably assure us of the magnitude of his devotion.

If God is *agape* as John says he is, then we can without any misinterpretation of scripture, read this Corinthian's passage the following way:

- *Your Father* is patient.
- *Your Father* is kind.
- *Your Father* does not envy.
- *Your Father* does not boast.
- *Your Father* is not proud.

- *Your Father* is not rude.
- *Your Father* is not self-seeking.
- *Your Father* is not easily angered.
- *Your Father* keeps no record of wrongs.
- *Your Father* does not delight in evil.
- *Your Father* rejoices with the truth.
- *Your Father* always protects.
- *Your Father* always trusts.
- *Your Father* always hopes.
- *Your Father* always perseveres.
- *Your Father* never fails.

It grieves me that at times, my perception of God's love has been so limited, and I've drifted from these simple yet profound truths. The question of agape really *is one of truth*. When a shred of doubt creeps in, just ask yourself, whose truth will you believe? Jesus said that God's word is truth! (John 17:17) Truth is always superlative to facts. Facts outside of scripture are always subject to change, and are subordinate to its truth; as a matter of fact, truth has the power to overturn the facts!

For example, let's suppose that twenty-five years ago a criminal was tried and convicted of murder. Though the man swore his innocence, a jury convicted him and a judge condemned him to die. *"Guilty, and death by execution."* However, six months before his execution, the court allows DNA testing, a relatively new forensics tool, to be applied to the evidence in his case.

This new knowledge produces truth that verifies his innocent plea years before. The case is reviewed and the man is exonerated. Society mourns the fact that a man was wrongly condemned. However, the facts of the original case are still the same. He was tried, convicted, and sentenced for murder; facts recorded in federal court records. This man would have wrongly died if *truth* had not come forth, changed the facts, and expunged his guilty record.

Isn't the same true today for us as we meditate on Paul's words to the Corinthian church? The facts may be that we have experienced love in ways that are far inferior to first Corinthians chapter thirteen.

My question to you is this. Will you surrender the facts of your experience, the facts of brokenness and sometimes-unbearable pain, to be gloriously shattered and by the truth of God's agape that is pursuing you with a holy vigilance?

Yes, his agape is a passionate verb that takes amazing steps to deliver his children when life seems hopeless and all is lost.

A moving example of this kind of passion is found in a story about the life of Sir Oliver Cromwell.

During the 17th century, Oliver Cromwell, Lord Protector of England, sentenced a soldier to be shot for his crimes. The execution was to take place at the ringing of the evening curfew bell. However, the bell did not sound. The soldier's fiancé had climbed into the belfry and clung to the great clapper of the bell to prevent it from striking. When she was summoned by Cromwell to account for her actions, she wept as she showed him her bruised and bleeding hands. Cromwell's heart was touched and he said, "Your lover shall live because of your sacrifice. Curfew shall not ring tonight!"[8]

Like this passionate fiancé who risked her life to save her love…God's agape is aggressively pursuing you!

I have often associated *love* with the passive and soft idea that pop culture and Valentines Day has portrayed it to be. However, at this point in my walk of faith, I am convinced that God's love is the single most aggressive force in the universe.

Field Marshal Ferdinand Foch, a French soldier and writer, said that t*he most powerful weapon on earth is the human soul* *on fire.*[9] And when the human soul is ablaze with the pure love of God, watch out.

In 1 John 4:18 we are told that perfect love casts out fear. We know that Satan is the author and personification of that fear. Jesus tells us that Satan fell like lighting from heaven. (Luke 10:18) In a nanosecond, Satan was and then was not there.

My premise is this. Contrary to what may be established thought, I don't think it was God's *anger* that expelled Satan from Heaven after his rebellion. No, I believe it was the greatest tsunami wave of *agape* that the universe had ever seen. It was agape that cast Lucifer and one third of the angelic host from Heaven's borders. God's love for everything good, pure, and pristine demanded Satan's banishment from our Father's house.

It makes perfect sense to believe that as God forbade fear to dwell in his presence there, that he will certainly forbid it to dwell in the lives of his children here. Remember, we are the temple of his Holy Spirit. Please hear the Apostle Paul's exhortation to young Timothy as he encourages Timothy to press on through the difficulties and uncertainties of his first pastorate. "God has not given us the spirit of fear, but one of power, love, and a sound mind!"

In the John 4 passage mentioned earlier, John declares that he who is in fear has *one* major unresolved issue; he has not been made perfect or complete by the power of God's agape love. In other words, if we indeed live in fear, then we are unconvinced of our Father's constant *unconditional*, *undiminished* and *unrelenting* love for us.

This is deep stuff. We are living in an age of fear, fear for how we'll survive in a shaky economy, fear for our children in a perverted and unsafe world, we fear for the next tragedy that will come across the six o'clock news.

You and I cannot obtain this kind of love that ejects fear on our own, even with the world's highest education nor its best life coaches. Agape is received as a gift. God so loved that he gave.

Part of the aftermath inherent in our Adamic nature is our inability to experience agape. We love conditionally and reciprocate conditionally. It is not that we intend to love this way, but we are limited by our carnality, our human-ness.

We've missed the *love boat* because at best, we tend to give and receive love through the brokenness of performance-based acceptance. Performance based love is the Petri dish—that shallow cylindrical dish that biologists use to culture cells—of fear. When we strive for acceptance through what we do, rather than what we are, our fear cells start to multiply. Fear breeds fear.

Fear always makes the wolf bigger than it is.

It's a no "win-win" in any other love besides agape. We see the countless statistics of agape's absence all around us, validated by too many divorce courts, sad songs and broken lives. Yes, it sounds too depressing, and it would seem hopeless if it weren't for our secret weapon.

Child of God, I will let you in on an amazing truth. Love is fear's worst enemy! I once believed that the antidote for fear was to pray for more faith. After all, the writer of Hebrews tell us that the just shall *live* by faith? We do indeed live by faith; however, Paul tells us that faith works, flows, and is sustained by *love*.

The answer to a heart full of fear *is not faith*, but a baptism in the wonderful agape love of God.

Fear comes from uncertainty, and when we are certain of God's love, of our worth to him, we are almost impervious to fear. It silently leaves us when we embrace the truth that God is our Father and has only the best intentions for us. Love removes fear.

Have you ever seen a young child startled by something? Usually, the first thing she does is run for safety to mommy or daddy's arms. What happens next is amazing to behold. Not too long after being in a parent's embrace, her tears subside, and she opens up again to the world around her. Whatever the "it" they feared goes away, or the child is now certain the "it" will not hurt them again.

In this interaction, all mom or dad did was hold the child close. They didn't give little Johnny a lengthy list of faith-building scriptures or dissect the reason for Susie's anxiety. They simply offered a giant hug inviting their child to bury her head in a sheltering embrace. We all know, but are often oblivious to the *how* of what happens next. I submit to you that an invisible transaction of love occurs between the spirit of the parent and the spirit of the child.

All fear soon dissipates. Suddenly, with the monsters all gone, the child is again ready to engage the world. If you're a parent, you've seen this happen over and over again. Agape love between parent and child.

And what far greater measure of agape is awaiting your reception in the Heavenly Father's arms! He so wants to release a mighty wave of his love in you, and drive every trace of anxiety from the borders of your life. His love is the answer to the anxiety of provision. His love is the answer to the uncertainty of the future. His arms are open for you to run into and be sheltered in eternal embrace.

Once you drop your guard and invite his passion to permeate every pore of your existence, your perception of him will forever change. Not only will you view him through the lens of all the good that that scripture declares he is, you will begin to believe that all his promises are possible and available for you.

I believe that he is looking at us daily as we walk through life. He knows the things that terrify us, make us loose sleep and rob us of our peace. Abba Father yearns for us to cleave close to him when life is scary and nestle us there until all our fears are gone. His love is perfect; furthermore, it has never failed anyone who ran into its harbor for safety.

Remember his love is: *Unconditional*, *Undiminished*, and *Unrelenting*! I declare again, "Behold what manner of *love* the *Father* has bestowed on us, that we should be called *children* of God! (1 John 3:1 NKJV)

Maybe you are like me and in an time of great wounding or fear, you assumed inner vows of self-protection and self-preservation.

It is here that you must come face to face with words of Jesus in Matthew 16:25, *"Whoever desires to save his life will lose it, but whoever will lose his life for my sake will save it"*

At thirty-three years old, I finally gave up the reigns of my life's destiny. I left corporate America and all the imaginary security it could afford. I decided to cease from running from the call on my life as God beckoned me to join him in a great adventure of ministering his grace and love to others. I packed up my office and left corporate America on March 21, 2001, and I have never looked back.

Since then I have seen Father God's astounding provision for my family and ministry in ways that can only be described as miraculous. In the last ten years, God has provided for my family and me much better than I could do on my own. Through his wonderful saints, in addition to daily needs of finances, the Father has provided an SUV that perfectly met our needs, and we were given a fantastic home in a beautiful neighborhood in Birmingham. There is great provision, protection, and blessing for you as well, if you will surrender your rights as master of your life.

When we release our right to provide for ourselves and entrust our lives to the promises of his unfailing word, we indeed experience the reality of Philippians 4:19; But my God shall supply all your need according to his riches in glory by Christ Jesus. How this happens is amazing to experience!

Chapter 5

Birthright and Barter

And because we are his sons, God has sent the Spirit of his Son into our hearts, so now we can rightly speak of God as our dear Father. Now we are no longer slaves but God's own sons. And since we are his sons, <u>everything</u> <u>he</u> <u>has</u> <u>belongs</u> <u>to</u> <u>us</u>, for that is the way God planned.
(Galatians 4:6-7 TLB)

Christ has redeemed us from the curse of the law, having become a curse for us (for it is written, "Cursed is everyone who hangs on a tree") that the blessing of Abraham might come upon the Gentiles in Christ Jesus, that we might receive the promise of the Spirit through *faith*.
(Galatians 3:13-14)

I n Genesis 25, we read the revealing story of Jacob, Esau and the stolen birthright. When Jacob deceived his father, he knew exactly what he was doing. Birthright was, (and still is), everything when it comes to provision. The definition of birthright is this: *a right or privilege you are entitled to at birth. Heritage, inheritance, any attribute or immaterial possession inherited from ancestors.* It is also means that which is inherited, a title or property or estate that passes by law to the heir on the death of the owner. Because we are Americans, freedom is our birthright.

In Jacob's time, birthright meant that the first-born son received a double portion of inheritance and headship in the family tree. And, in his case, a forever fellowship and blessing with the covenant God. Jacob desperately wanted the privileges of birthright. Through his twin brother Esau's ignorance and impulsiveness, he won it. Esau foolishly sold his birthright to Jacob for a meal.

What made the birthright so desirable was that the *constitution* behind birthright was God's unalterable covenant. Covenant in simple terms means an agreement—a promise—between God and his people.

The first mention of covenant in the Bible is found in Genesis 6:8, when God promises to spare Noah from the impending flood. The covenant was an act of God's grace. Later, in Exodus, God made covenants with Abraham, Isaac, Jacob, and then the nation of Israel through Moses. As we know, Israel lacked the heart to obey God and they were in constant turmoil as they wandered seeking the Promised Land. Covenant then and now, is the power in the earth that enforces birthright benefits for God's children.

Much like Esau, through envy, pride and ignorance, Lucifer forfeited his eternal rights of blessing and fellowship with the Father. Never forget that he lives to make you do the same. As we talked about in chapter two, he is after our identity, because identity has inheritance connected to it.

What does this inheritance look like? First, let's remember that we are children of God under the New Covenant—where God promises to put his laws into our mind and write them on our hearts. (Hebrews 8:10) The New Covenant is better than the first. It promises us the power to obey God through the indwelling of the Holy Spirit.

It's our birthright; but amazingly, not reserved only for the first-born.

Through Jesus our elder brother, the Father assured that all his children could enjoy identical birthright privileges. Jesus was not selfish and did the unthinkable for a first-born Hebrew male. He willingly gave up exclusivity to the birthright, so the rest of his siblings could participate in it equally.

Consider Paul's words to the church at Ephesus. "*Blessed be the God and Father of our Lord Jesus Christ, who has blessed us with every spiritual blessing in the heavenly places in Christ Jesus.*" (Ephesians 1:3) What an exciting and wonderful word—us. It implies you, me, them and every other child of God who would be adopted into his family.

Now, before we go any further, let me take five minutes to distinguish between Jesus' position as the Son of God, and our redemptive sonship and its benefits.

Jesus is unique in that, he and only he, is the Father's *only begotten* Son. It is he who is co-equal in the Trinity with the Father and the Holy Spirit. This redemptive sonship that I will discuss in this chapter is not equal to Jesus' "only begotten sonship." Being the only begotten of the Father is exclusive to Jesus and it is an eternal *position* that is his alone. Redemptive sonship is available to all who are redeemed by his substitutionary work at Calvary, and it affords *participation in the benefits* that Jesus the Son has always enjoyed.

Our redemptive sonship is one of the great lessons in the book of Revelation. John portrays the redeemed sons of God as the ones who throw their crowns down before the Father. It is the Father, along with the Lamb, who are the ones qualified to sit on Heaven's greatest thrones.

The redeemed and adopted sons are those who worship and adore forever the only begotten Son and His Father. Redeemed sons is an incredible status; because through grace, we can become like the only begotten son in character and conduct; however, we are *not* the *only begotten's* equal, or even close to His equal.

Jesus the Son went back to heaven and now sits in regal and eternal splendor at the Father's right hand. As I pointed out, one of the elements of His job description is as our Intercessor. The adopted sons can approach His throne with confidence, but they will never attain the right to sit on His throne.

Since Joseph is an Old Testament type of Christ, perhaps Joseph's story is a good word picture to lay the foundation of what I need to communicate here. Joseph loved his brethren and wanted to reconcile with them the first time he saw them. He also showed them agape love, doing what was best for them when they clearly could not help themselves, nor did they deserve help. He even coached them in how to ask Pharaoh for

Goshen. The love was the same, the relationship as brothers was the same, and Joseph was not ashamed to call them brethren.

However, the brothers' positions, privileges, authority, wealth, and access to Pharaoh were not at all the same.

Only Joseph at this point was going sit on a throne beside Pharaoh and his brothers would be subservient - a foreshadowing of Jesus and the Father in eternity, and how we all will bow down and worship at their thrones!

Okay, moving forward, and hopefully having a proper frame of reference, what then do our benefits as sons of God look like and how do we access them? In order to believe the fullness of Ephesians 1:3, that we have "been blessed with every spiritual blessing in Heavenly places," we need to explore some truths that may seem unbelievable or possibly uncomfortable to your theology.

Child of God, you need to know that your Father feels the same way about you and me as he does about Jesus. Let me rephrase that...*God loves you and me as much as he loves Jesus!* What? Huh? Can this be? This statement seems sacrilegious and unbelievable, but we can validate it completely through scripture. Let's meditate on the following passages:

For it was fitting for him, in whom are all things and by whom are all things, in *bringing many sons to glory*, to make the captain of their salvation perfect through sufferings. *For* **both He who sanctifies** *and* **those who are being sanctified** **are all of one**, for which reason *He is not ashamed to call them brethren*, 12 saying: "*I will declare Your name to My brethren…*

(Hebrews 2:10-12)

For whom He foreknew, He also predestined to be conformed to the image of his Son, that He might be the **firstborn** among *many brethren*.

(Romans 8:29)

… But you received the Spirit of adoption by whom we cry out, "Abba, Father." 16 The Spirit Himself bears witness with our spirit that we are children of God, 17 *and if children, then heirs — heirs of God and* **joint heirs** *with Christ…*

(Romans 8:15-17)

God designed our redemption plan through Christ to ensure that all of humanity could be become heirs with Christ. I like how the Message version of the Bible explains Romans 8:29:

"God knew what he was doing from the very beginning. He decided from the outset to shape the lives of those who love him along the same lines as the life of his Son." The Apostle Paul underscores this truth by declaring that not only are we heirs, but we are *joint heirs*.

Those two words change everything. Have you ever held a joint-checking account? If so, you can better appreciate what Paul is saying. Joint account holders have equal privileges with the same account at their financial institution.

Lisa can make debits, credits, or even withdrawals on every penny in our account. We are equal partners in everything. What I have is hers and vice-versa. And we, being joint-heirs with Christ, not only get a portion of God's inheritance, we receive an equal share of this inheritance. This means joint access to all of the Father's blessings; his grace, love, loyalty, redemption, emotional healing and every other good and perfect gift. This sounds a lot like, "...Every spiritual blessing in heavenly places," as found in Ephesians 1:3.

It's amazing how God can do this. More so, why would he do this? The simple answer is simple indeed; he wants to. Done, decided. However, I want you to know there is sound theology to verify the fact that as the Father chose to treat Jesus by his Spirit; He chooses to deal likewise with us.

If Jesus is the first born of many brethren—and God deals with all his kids equally—then we can expect our Father to interact with us as he did with Jesus. Remember, the New Testament reminds us that God is no respecter of persons. He is just and equitable in the way he deals with us.

It seems like a bit of a spiritual stretch, doesn't it?

The following scriptural constructs are not exhaustive on this subject, but are crucial to accept if we dare believe that we have the same birthright as Jesus, our elder brother. The way to bring this home is to study these passages and ask the Holy Spirit to confirm them in your heart. After all, he wrote them.

Satan has blinded much of the body of Christ to these eternal truths through timid or erroneous pulpits, and their omission is obvious in much of seminary curriculum. He knows that if all churches embrace and implement these truths, his mission is ruined.

In the diverse culture in which we live and worship, many denominations resist the concept that we have as much access to God and his blessings as Jesus did. *Of course, we are not divine*; this goes without saying, but our spirits are reborn through Christ, and we are eternal children with divine privileges as joint heirs.

As I began my healing process in learning to be a son, I continually asked the Holy Spirit to renew my mind with these truths.

- **Jesus was fathered by the Spirit:** "...and the angel answered and said to her, "the Holy Spirit will come upon you, and the power of the Highest will overshadow you; therefore, also, that Holy one who is to be born will be called the son of God. (Luke 1:35-36)
- **We have been fathered by the Spirit:** "...And because you are sons, *God has sent forth the Spirit of his Son into your hearts, crying out, "Abba, Father!"* Therefore you are no longer a slave but a son, and if a son, then an heir of God through Christ. (Galatians 4:6-9)

Yes, the Great Jehovah has fathered us, and we are now his offspring with Divine DNA infused and imprinted into our spirits. We are in his likeness and show forth his nature. By virtue of this bestowal, we have a commission to bring many other sons to glory. We are joint heirs that are making heavenly deposits by laying up treasures in Heaven, where moth and dust cannot corrupt.

If Jesus were speaking those words to us today, he'd be telling us to store up our treasures where they won't be destroyed by what our culture claims is worth pursuing. All the earthly treasures we work for are temporary, and the mad chase after them rarely brings long lasting contentment.

We are new creations who lavish our praise and worship on Jesus, who in turn daily loads our accounts with spiritual benefits and divine disbursements. And often, they come in the form of material gain which we are prompted to use for God's glory. We have been forever sealed by his Holy Spirit as God's own children:

- **Jesus was sealed by the Spirit** "...do not labor for the food which perishes, but for the food which endures to everlasting life, which the son of man will give you, *because God the Father has set his seal on him.*" (John 6:27)
- **We are sealed by the Spirit**: "., in whom also, having believed, *you were sealed with the Holy Spirit of promise* who is the guarantee of our inheritance... (Ephesians 1:13-14) The Lord knows who are his.

Think of the great seal of the United States—the bald eagle with its wings outstretched holding those thirteen arrows in his left talon—an olive branch in the other; above him the scroll with the motto *E pluribus Unum, "Out of Many, One."*

This seal authenticates all official U.S. documents. It is embossed on our passports and ensures our embarkation as we travel, and then or safe reentry to the United States' sovereign borders. The seal or logo of any great company gives the product identity and authenticity; it distinguishes their product or service with something we call "branding," or customer recognition. Who doesn't recognize the Starbucks™ logo when we see it on a paper coffee cup?

And we instantly know it's *Disney,* the largest media and entertainment conglomerate in the world, by the simple font that reads, *The Walt Disney Company.*™ God's seal upon us identifies us as his own. It validates our existence as his chosen generation and royal priesthood.

So we are eternally branded with his holy insignia. His blood shouts our identity to the unseen realm as we declare his name to all that is visible. This seal endures and ensures our ultimate redemption, where one day our corruptible bodies will don immortality.

- ***Jesus was anointed by the Spirit:*** *"…*how *God anointed Jesus of Nazareth with the Holy Spirit* and with power, who went about doing good and healing all who were oppressed by the devil, for God was with him. (Acts 10:38-39)

- ***We are anointed by his Spirit…"…*now he who establishes us with you in Christ *and has anointed us is God.* (2 Corinthians 1:20-22) *But the anointing which you have received from him abides in you…* (1 John 2:27)

The anointing is the power of God in us to accomplish the purposes of God on the earth. The New Testament Greek word for anoint is *chriô.* In Bible times people were anointed with oil to signify God's blessing or call on that person's life. They participated in anointing ceremonies where they were set apart, given their commissions authorized by God to go out and do his work. In 1 John 2:20 we are told that every Christian possesses the holy anointing. *"But you have an anointing from the Holy One, and all of you know the truth."* (NIV) Another word for "anointed" means "chosen one."

You have been chosen by God, anointed for a special purpose. And you have your own individual anointing of the Holy Spirit that when he comes to live in you. Understanding this anointing will break the yolks of ignorance and barriers of opposition. If we know that we are anointed to perpetuate the work that Jesus began, it will energize and excite us. This anointing will continue to flow until all of the earth is filled with his glory.

Acts 10:38 tells us that the Father anointed Jesus to go about and do good, healing all who were oppressed of the devil. This same anointing abides in us to continue to set captives free and do even greater works than Jesus did. How you are gifted to *set the captives* free may be vastly different from the way God has gifted me.

I have a passion to reach the lost through speaking. As an evangelist and teacher from the core, it's natural for me to speak, whether it's in Africa or in intimate settings where Lisa and I minister each month during Bible studies. Proverbs 18:16 tells us that our gifts will make room for us, even if the places seem unlikely or even incomprehensible.

Recently, I found myself with a ministry team in Sierra Leone, West Africa. We had travelled to Sierra Leone for a mission's initiative and had a serendipitous experience. We ended up having an unscheduled audience with the President, His Excellency Dr. Ernest Bai Koroma and his wife, First Lady Sia Koroma. Per their invitation, we ministered and prophesied over these leaders and their nation. I'm sure none of us will ever forget that moment. Regardless of where God places me, His anointing flows and the words come.

You may be anointed to shepherd others or teach in some capacity, or you may just love to serve or share your gift of mercy. Though you may never have taken a spiritual gifts inventory, you have a sense of what your gifts are. They come from deep within you. They give you passion, they propel you. Why? Because God is forever seeking to manifest himself through you.

As God chose to deal with Jesus, he will choose to deal with us. Not only are we fathered, sealed, and anointed by The Spirit, we learn to die to self by the Spirit.

- **Jesus allowed his crucifixion by the Spirit**, and by his Spirit we are cleansed from our sin. His sacrifice changed our lives, transformed our hearts. Nothing we do can stifle this work. *"How much more shall the blood of Christ, who through the eternal Spirit, offered himself without spot to God, cleanse your conscience from dead works to serve the living God?"* (Hebrews 9:14-15)

- **We crucify our flesh by the Spirit**. Romans 8:13 says, *For if you live according to the flesh you will die; but* *if by the Spirit you put to death the deeds of the body, you will live.* By his spirit we are delivered from that old life. We bury it, and as the Message says, "We move on."

How precious in the sight of the Lord is the death of his saints. He modeled death, even death unto the cross. The sobering question about this similitude is one that Jesus asked. *"Is the servant any greater than his master?"* Is our call to crucifixion to self any less commanded as his was?

Paul told us *"that as many of us that have been baptized have been baptized unto his death...these are his own."* However, know this precious child of God; *coffins cannot stay closed in the presence of Jesus.* He is The Resurrection and The Life! If we die with him, we are also raised in his power; furthermore, we are commissioned and empowered to bring resurrection life to all around us!

Okay, though the comparisons do not stop here, surely you can grasp the parallels. So then, *if* God by his Spirit has been so intentional to treat us as he did Jesus, why would it be a stretch to assume that we have the same birthright as the Son enjoys? Friend, it is not stretch but a guarantee.

God did not want us to stumble upon this truth. He chose to place Jesus, the culmination of all his covenants, and the source of the new birthright, in our hearts. He desired that we walk in these truths and their inherent blessings continuously! Abba Father deliberately wants you to know that through Christ, you are now a beneficiary of all the good promised or alluded to by every covenant promise. God is so deliberate about this, that 2 Corinthians 1:20 tells us ...*For **all** the promises of God in him are Yes, and in him Amen, to the glory of God through us.*

Remember, those promises are assured through covenant, which again, is the constitution that underwrites our birthright.

Since the beginning of his interaction with humanity, God has implemented covenants to detail the scope of his promises towards his own. He built a people and a family. Jesus, the author and finisher of the New Covenant, is the embodiment of the fullness of all of God's promises. If you have made Christ your savior and Lord, he and covenant power dwells in you.

You might think that all sounds wonderful and spiritual, but how can we understand this New Covenant in a very practical way? There are multiple covenants throughout the Bible; in fact, God's Word is a book of covenants more than it is anything else.

I wish I had the knowledge to fully explore the depths of covenant teaching. However, let me provide a quick overview of the concept and illuminate just some of what our birthright includes.

In ancient times, covenants were primarily cut for three reasons; mutual protection, provision, or blessing between clans, tribes and even nations. However, the ways they were instituted were varied.

The gist of the rituals would go something like this:

- The representative heads of two tribes or clans of people would bring their peoples together.
- The covenant ceremony would begin by the leaders exchanging their names...*i.e.*, the clan of *Potter* joining you, the clan of *Reader*.
- From now until eternity, our people will be known as *Potter-Reader* and you, *Reader-Potter*, thus giving us identity as one.
- We then would exchange our cloaks/tunics as symbol to our peoples that whatever personal belongings we had, would be jointly ours.
- Often following garments would be a swapping of crops or goods. If my clan excelled as farmers of grain, we

would offer a portion to you and you would offer your main crop to us.

- This would be a pledge to our people that we are given the freedom to walk freely into your fields at any time of need or want, and the same would be true for you and yours.
- Finally, there would be an exchange of weapons. We might be fierce with the spear and you with the bow. This exchange told our enemies that if they ever attacked the clan of "Reader," they had just picked a fight with "Potter."

After all this occurred, to seal the stipulations of the covenant, there would be a recitation of blessings declared from each representative head over the opposite clan. Conversely, there would be a recitation of curses to come upon the joint tribes if covenant agreements were broken in any way.

If you read Deuteronomy 28 you'll see the blessing elements clearly in the first fourteen verses. "Your town and fields will be blessed, your children and your crops...the offspring of your herds and flock...." The latter fifty-three verses outline the curses.

"Confusion and frustration in everything you do…" These include defeats by your enemies, boils, tumors and scurvy, and locusts devouring your crops. Not a pretty sight.

Often the covenants were sealed by a mingling of blood of the designated leadership, through a physical *cutting* ceremony, a symbol of the forever promise; their respective peoples and future generations had now become one.

To culminate the covenant, a huge meal and celebration between the parties ratified the ceremony and sealed it in perpetuity.

Why would I bother to share all this with you, you might wonder.

It's a symbol of our amazing barter:

We give in return for something received. Giving and receiving reciprocally. *The rites found in ancient covenant making are foreshadowing our ultimate covenant with God our Father through Christ Jesus, our Savior and Lord.*

Please allow me elaborate. When you accepted Christ, your name was changed. Not your given name, but what you are forever called in God's eyes. You transformed from being a slave and outsider, to belonging as his child and heir.

Those with a slave mindset are like orphans, feeling like they are unworthy to sit at father God's table of provision. They live by a works-based (performance-based) salvation, always trying to earn a place in Father's heart. Sons and daughters however, know that they have a right to sit at father's table because of grace and grace alone.

In this swapping process, you also had a holy *exchange of garments*. You traded your best spiritual suit—which Scripture says amounts to filthy rags—for his spotless and holy robe of righteousness. And it cloaks you continually.

Next, your net worth of resources expounded beyond measure. As you offer him one tenth of your increase—which is what God asks for in Malachi chapter 3 verse 10, he turns around and swaps this for *"all your needs being supplied according to his riches in Glory by Christ Jesus. As Paul old us in Philippians 4:19"* You are now a joint-heir to incalculable spiritual blessings and surplus according to Ephesians chapter 1:3.

You also received *a new arsenal* for warfare, second to none as given to us in 2 Corinthians 10:4 *"The weapons of our warfare are not carnal, but mighty through God to pulling down every stronghold of the enemy…"* This arsenal gives you and me supernatural insight and power of how to effectively break through every mental and spiritual barrier that hinders us from walking in the abundant life Jesus promised.

The devil's best weapons are distractions—which we battle daily in our busy world—and discouragement, which is rampant today in our shaky financial climate.

As I addressed in Chapter 3, the world is obsessed by fear. Fear is written in large print on human hearts and faces everywhere you look. It's what keeps the news broadcasting twenty-four hours a day. We fear diseases and poverty and terrorists and nuclear war. We fear letting our kids play in the front yard and on the computer screen anymore.

Psychologist's offices and Xanax bottles are both filled to overflowing as people seek some solace for their minds tormented by anxiety. Yet, as God's sons and daughters, we aren't subject to fear anymore. We are in a covenant relationship with the living God. His spirit reigns within us. This is amazing for sure, but it gets even better.

To sanction the covenant, blood needed to be spilled. All through the Word of God we see that without the shedding of blood, sins could not be atoned. Your blood was not good enough and mine *certainly* was not. The law of sin demanded death, and humanity needed a hero to come to our rescue. Thank God, that he sent Jesus who willingly laid his life down for all who would accept salvation. Listen and rejoice in the benediction of Hebrews:

"Now may the God of peace who brought up our Lord Jesus from the dead, that great Shepherd of the sheep, *through the blood of the everlasting covenant*, make you complete in every good work to do his will, working in you what is well pleasing in his sight, through Jesus Christ, to whom be glory forever and ever. Amen." (13:20-21)

His blood was and is forever sufficient. Also through Christ, the Father permanently dealt with the curses and blessings portion of covenant making. Keeping the covenant is impossible for us to do.

When the covenant was broken, the curse was real and severe. However, Galatians 3:13-14 reminds us that Christ redeemed each of us from all the curses of the broken covenant. While we don't see plagues like those of old, we face modern afflictions that keep us from prospering. The blessings that were promised from Abraham to Christ can now be ours. This fact comforts me greatly when the enemy mocks that God is still El Shaddai, our all sufficient provider.

Each time we take communion, the ancient covenant celebration meal is ratified and foreshadowed, but ultimately will culminate at the marriage supper of the Lamb. What makes all this relevant to you? What qualifies you to benefit in God's covenants from Abraham forward? What ensures you that you and every other child of God have identical birth right benefits?

The following scriptures reveal the answer.

"And I will establish My covenant between Me and you and your descendants after you in their generations, for an everlasting covenant, to be God to you and your descendants after you." (Genesis 17:7)

"For he is not a Jew who is one outwardly, nor is circumcision that which is outward in the flesh; 29 but he is a Jew who is one inwardly; and circumcision is that of the heart, in the Spirit, not in the letter; whose praise is not from men but from God. (Romans 2:28-29)

Christ has redeemed us from the curse of the law, having become a curse for us (for it is written, "Cursed is everyone who hangs on a tree") that the blessing of Abraham might come upon the Gentiles in Christ Jesus, that we might receive the promise of the Spirit through faith.

(Galatians 3:13-14)

The divine blessing will never fail. Can it get more reassuring than that? I pray these verses will cause you to have a spectacular spiritual identity crisis. Child of God let me assure you, if you have made Christ your Savior and Lord, you are now a Hebrew and covenant heir. Paul tells the church in Rome, and everyone else who would receive Christ as Lord, that we are all now Israelites in the sight of God. Furthermore, we are birthright beneficiaries, all eligible and qualified to participate in these abundant blessings.

How I hope you will let these truths become a daily reality in your relationship with God through Christ. These are the linchpins of son and daughtership. As you synthesize them and they become your identity, you will begin to walk in a fullness of joy and blessing far-beyond what your have previously experienced as a believer.

If Esau had taken the time to consider his inheritance, he never would have made such a rash decision to sell his birthright for a bowl of stew. He failed to grasp the worth of his birthright, to properly discern what was truly important. He sacrificed his future on the altar of immediate gratification.

There is a great lesson for us in this story. When we let the common things of the world consume us, we miss our blessing. The world rushes on today faster than ever, and it gives little thought to God or eternal things. We - God's children, need to remember to whom we belong and let our lives reflect this awareness.

That said, thus far in this volume, it has been my objective to develop the great truth the Lord showed me after a night in prayer: God was not calling me to be a great man of God, but to be a son of God. In this position of a covenant heir, and in a posture of expectancy to receive what God has promised, one of the most difficult challenges we can face is how to balance the blessings of birthright and walk in humility as his servants.

I once heard it said that gratitude is the rent we pay for being born. There is no greater *payment* we can offer our Father than returning our lives in grateful service to him and his kingdom. For the rest of our time together, we will begin to examine what this high and lofty position of sonship entails and how to practically live it out in our fallen world.

Chapter 6

Greatness, Gifts, Grasslands and Gymnasiums

Jesus, knowing that the Father had given all things into his hands, and that He had come from God and was going to God, rose from supper and laid aside his garments, took a towel and girded Himself. After that, He poured water into a basin and began to wash the disciples' feet

(John 13:3-5)

But he who is greatest among you shall be your servant. And whoever exalts himself will be humbled, and he who humbles himself will be exalted.

(Matthew 23:11-12)

I'm a big fan of the Rocky movies. One night I popped in Rocky IV where the *Italian Stallion*, played by Sylvester Stallone, comes out of retirement to battle the Russian heavyweight, the steroid-powered Ivan Drago. One of my favorite scenes, is where Apollo Creed is training Rocky for the fight to reclaim his title as heavyweight champion. Apollo, trying to dissuade Rocky from fighting again, tells him to stay in school and use his brain. "Be a doctor, a lawyer, carry a leather suitcase. Forget about sports. Be a thinker, not a stinker."

As their dialogue progresses, Rocky has some fun with Apollo as they verbally spar with one another. Rocky informs his old opponent that he would have no chance against him if they ever went toe-to-toe in the ring again. As their sparring match ends, Apollo intently looks at the young fighter and says, "Remember...you fight great, but I'm a great fighter!"

Apollo's words embody the basic plot of all the Rocky series: A talented no name boxer pops up out of nowhere and gets a shot at being a champion.

I believe that Apollo's words *also* provide us the framework for two schools of thought regarding the origin of greatness. One side sees greatness as an overnight rise out of obscurity, of being thrust into limelight by uncommon talent and timing. The other sees greatness as a slow and often painful ascent, plodding through years of peppering by hard knocks, yet never shrinking back until success is achieved.

When it comes to prominence in the Kingdom of God, I'm convinced that our father often allows his children to train in the inglorious gym of *Apollo's* school of hard knocks and persistence.

Concerning greatness, it might surprise you that God has not called any of us to obtain it. What he *has* called us to, is to walk out this life in h-umility, o-bedience and e-xcellence. I like to think of these three virtues as a "HOE" that we all have access to. Regardless of our individual giftings, pedigree, and influence, the Lord wants us to implement these virtues as we cultivate the fields of our lives. I believe in this *tool* so confidently, that if you and I humbly obey the laws of any field or discipline, and do this with excellence—greatness is inevitable.

However, greatness in God's eyes is not a destination, but a journey, and how well we serve the needs of others as we take each step is a reflection of who we believe God is in our lives. It is interesting that in the day of mega ministries and lofty five-fold aspirations, many of God's people have lost touch with Jesus' idea of being great. The desire to abandon self and serve others seems so distant from much of what is prevalent in today's *Church of the Sensation and Gratification*. Even in many pulpits, there is a disparity between what Christ taught on servanthood and what is practiced by leadership.

Today everyone wants the spotlight, *but no one wants to change the bulb.*

Before I left corporate America, I was in a senior management position with several assistants on hand to take care of all the mundane things that kept our department running and organized. I attended to the big decisions.

I was in the driver's seat of all the major issues, the big-picture guy you might say. When I took my first ministry position, I just knew my amazing skill set would serve me quite well. Boy was I wrong. My boss and the ministry's founder, Steve Franklin, "allowed me" to transition from being a senior manager at a fortune company to serve as the ministry's janitor and head gopher. I went from making executive hiring decisions, to serving as CEO of the copy machine and the tape duplicator. One of my most important tasks of the day was ensuring ample toilet paper was available in the time of *need*.

Steve wouldn't allow me to teach or preach, not even one small message, until I had been with the ministry nearly a year. What audacity I thought. Was he *that* clueless to the gift he had been given in me, the former senior manager from a Fortune company?

I do hope you sense my sarcasm.

It took me awhile to realize what Steve clearly saw that I was blinded to. Humility and willingness to serve in anonymity is usually the sole preparation ground for promotion in God's Kingdom. I had a copious deficit of humility and had never relished the anonymity thing.

When I say humility, I am not referring to an abject groveling, self-deprecating spirit. True humility is simply the right estimate of ourselves as God sees us. What I see in the Gospels is that Jesus personified serving in anonymity, and the Father expects no less from his other children. As someone once said, the humble soul is a temple of God.

The first century believers certainly got the message. We find an excellent example of this kind of servanthood in the story of Acts chapter 6:1-6. The context of this passage surrounds Pentecost and the explosion of the early church. Many converts to Christianity remained in Jerusalem to be a part of this new religion that brought life and power to Abraham's children. Among the multitudes, there were a number of Jewish and Greek widows that needed care. The Apostles knew that these women, along with fatherless children, were (and still are) the heartbeat of true religion, so great attention was given to their care. Yet, there was also the urgent need for evangelism and church planting among the rest of the Jews.

The Apostles had to make some adjustments to enable the Great Commission to continue. It is in this story found in Acts 6:1-6 that we see how God honors servanthood and what I've come to call *"ministry in the mundane."*

During this time the disciples were increasing in number, growing by leaps and bounds. Murmurings started among the Greek believers because their widows were being neglected by the Hebrews in the daily food lines. So the twelve called a meeting and discussed the issue. They couldn't very well abandon their duties of preaching and teaching to care for all the poor, so they chose seven men "full of the Holy Spirit, and full of wisdom," to tend to this business. The 12 would stick to what they were called to do. "

And they chose Stephen, a man full of faith and the Holy Spirit, and Philip, Prochorus, Nicanor, Timon, Parmenas, and Nicolas, a proselyte from Antioch, whom they set before the apostles; and when they had prayed, they laid hands on them. (Acts 6:5-6)

The Apostles under the direction of the Holy Spirit then make a very interesting statement concerning servanthood. In essence they said: *We need seven men to be waiters and bus boys*. Now, the first thing that grips me in this passage is the resume' that these men had to possess to get the job. In God's eyes, the following qualifications are essential to bus tables at *The Apostles Café*.

- *You better have a good reputation and be living right*
- *You must be full of the Holy Spirit and Divine wisdom*
- *Oh, one more thing…your first day begins after the apostolic ordination service.*

Would you agree that God is extremely serious about servanthood?

Let's focus on the rest of the story for a minute. If you follow at least two of these men, you will see how their serving in relative obscurity must have caught God's attention.

Later in this chapter, we see Stephen begin his transformation from menial laborer to the first wonder-working martyr. Not long after, we find Phillip preaching, baptizing, and then teleporting through the sky! What happened? What was the key that caught the attention of the Father? Here is my opinion, and you don't have to agree. Oh, just to warn you, I need another five minutes back up on my soapbox. Here goes:

All of these men embraced the call to serve in a position that might fall well-beneath some of today's high profile ministers/ministries. You see, it was their privilege, their honor, and their duty to serve the widows. In their eyes, *serving God was indistinguishable from serving others.* Wow, has the 21st century Church lost that truth! Too much of what I see, at least in the charismatic wing of the Church, is so off-center from our first century roots. Sometimes, the behavior of believers and ministers makes me a bit nauseous.

Francois La Rochefoucals said that humility is the altar on which God wishes us to offer sacrifices to him. So very true.

Where is the abundance of humble servants like these men and their co-workers, Prochorus, Nicanor, Timon, Parmenas, and Nicolas? Where are people who are okay with serving in obscurity? I would dare to say our spiritual compass has lost true north. The full-gospel branch of ministry that I am mostly familiar with, has become so enamored with the *glamour* of ministry, that we have lost the *gut* of ministry.

There are multitudes that will spend hours at a conference to get a prophetic word, but will not spend thirty minutes reading or seeking to obey *the* Word. Sadly, we have become anointing junkies, personality junkies, but not Jesus Junkies.

Humor me a little more as I echo John Bevere for a moment. If I promoted a huge charismatic conference headlined by some big name prophets who might speak a personal "thus saith" to the attendees, I would likely gather a capacity crowd. However, if I concurrently held another conference, and the main agenda would be the fruit of the Spirit such as *longsuffering*, *patience*, and *self control*, and the breakout sessions were "nursery worker 101" and "bathroom cleanliness 202," the attendance would likely be dismal.

How did we get here? I believe it is because *gifts* have become superlative to *fruit*, and *anointing* is more valued than *character*.

This is amazing to me because the gifts of the Spirit are temporal; yet as I understand scripture, the fruit of the Spirit is eternal…"*Love will never fail, but where there are prophecies they will cease…*" That said, I personally believe that the fruit of the Spirit is equivalent with character and integrity. If we are to accurately demonstrate Christ to our broken world, we the children of God must be established and balanced on the two pillars of effective ministry: Christ-like character and Holy Spirit empowerment.

Concerning these pillars, allow me address a relevant truth that I believe is hidden in a "go to" passage for those of us who are Pentecostals. The latter part of Joel Chapter 2 is where we often go to validate God's Spirit that is being poured out again upon his church in these last days. I agree with this stance and believe and purport these verses. However, in verses 24 and 25 of this same chapter, Joel speaks about a great restoration of all that has been eaten off the *vine* by the "worms of destruction."

Now, I have heard numerous speakers expound on these two verses, often preaching that they allude to a great restoration of financial and material blessings coming back to the people of God in these last days as well.

Though I believe that God is a restorer and redeemer, I do not feel that this inference about financial restoration is the *heart* of this passage at all. I say this because the outpouring of God's Spirit and subsequent spiritual gifts, is what Joel is ultimately saying is going to happen in the last days. However, he says this outpouring will occur *after a great restoration*; but a restoration of what?

If we study the New Testament, we learn that there are nine gifts of the Spirit and nine fruit of the Spirit. As I said earlier, I believe that the fruit of the Spirit is tantamount with character and integrity. That said, verses 24 and 25 of this passage are regarding a restoration of what grows on the vine...and that my friends is *fruit*!

Prophetically, I believe that these "worms of destruction" are actually worms of sin and character compromise that have plagued the Church and its leadership throughout history.

As the Song of Solomon says, it is the little foxes that destroy the vine. (15:2) I say that it is the little compromises of character which ultimately spoil the minister and believer and make our fruit *inedible*!

Concerning the pillars of giftings and character, I believe that Joel's prophetic latter day passage is as much about a restoration of spiritual fruit, (Christ-like character), as it is about an outpouring of gifts in God's children and his church. This demonstration of power and purity will make an indisputable statement to the world of Christ's authenticity in us, and his delivering power that is available for them.

This balance of power with integrity is what we need to correct the spiritual "bipolar" condition of many who have evidence of the Spirit, yet do not live out the character produced by its truth. Jesus said our Father is seeking worshippers who would have both.

Concerning gifts, if we are not careful, we could be inclined to assume that they by themselves are validation of the Father's approval. This is not necessarily true. Let me direct you to the words of Jesus to elaborate my point further. In Matthew chapters 5-7, Jesus gives us the Sermon on the Mount. Two of the most sobering passages of scripture in all of the Bible are found in chapter 7, verses 15-23.

These passages are rarely discussed, much less preached about, as they cause great uneasiness for those of us who are "full-gospel." Listen to the words of Jesus as he approaches the end of his sermon on the mount.

"Beware of false prophets, who come to you in sheep's clothing, but inwardly they are ravenous wolves. *You will know them by their fruits*. Do men gather grapes from thorn bushes or figs from thistles? Even so, every good tree bears good fruit, but a bad tree bears bad fruit. *A good tree cannot bear bad fruit, nor can a bad tree bear good fruit*. Every tree that does not bear good fruit is cut down and thrown into the fire. *Therefore by their fruits you will know them*. "Not everyone who says to Me, 'Lord, Lord,' shall enter the kingdom of heaven, but he who does the will of My Father in heaven."

Many will say to Me in that day, *'Lord, Lord, have we not prophesied in Your name, cast out demons in Your name, and done many wonders in Your name?'* And then I will declare to them, 'I never knew you; depart from Me, you who practice lawlessness!' (Matthew 7:15-23)

Isn't it interesting that the "flavor" of Christianity that Jesus addresses in this passage is not Southern Baptist, Presbyterian, Episcopalian, or even Catholicism.

In this stern admonition, Jesus specifically addresses the ministry that is practiced and propagated by those of us who identify ourselves as Pentecostal or Charismatic. Jesus knew that if we were not discerning, we would believe that *the anointing of God is synonymous with the approval of God.* Again, this is not necessarily the case, though many of my Pentecostal friends may strongly disagree with that statement. The anointing of God has always been poured out upon imperfect clay vessels.

We see great character deficiencies in many Biblical heroes such as, Samson, Saul, and David. For example, in Judges Chapter 16, Samson demonstrates one of his greatest feats of strength under the anointing. Judges 16:3 tells us, "and Samson lay low till midnight; then he arose at midnight, took hold of the doors of the gate of the city and the two gateposts, pulled them up, bar and all, put them on his shoulders, and carried them to the top of the hill that faces Hebron."

Some scholars say that he uprooted these huge gates, pillars and all, and carried them for nearly forty-five minutes over his head while scaling Mount Hebron. Interestingly, my

Sunday school teacher failed to tell me that this incredible feat of anointed strength occurred right after he had been *lying with a prostitute* for half of the night. I guess there was no flannel graph caricature for that part of the story huh? We see similar character issues with other greatly anointed men such as Saul, David, Solomon, etc.

However, this idea of great anointing with questionable character is not just an Old Testament phenomenon.

Remember in Matthew 10:8, that Judas, who Jesus would later say "was a devil," was one of the twelve that Jesus sent out to preach the Gospel, heal the sick, and cleanse the lepers. And Peter, who Jesus had to rebuke Satan's influence over as Jesus' crucifixion was drawing near, would also be one of the firebrands God used to establish the Church. It is critical to note that in this Matthew chapter seven discourse, Jesus addresses the essential need for spiritual fruit in those who minister, but he also calls for fruit inspection among us as well.

Therefore, the gifts of The Spirit are indicative of what God *can do* through us, but the fruit of The Spirit is representative of *who he is* in us.

Oh for the day when our fruit is as matured as our gifts.

We have many in the church who are enamored with titles and their inherent privileges. People have often inferred that

I move in the office of a prophet. I tread very lightly at this designation and have not "worn" the title, and let me tell you why. Scripture only records one instance where a man *called himself* a prophet. It's found in 1 Kings 13:18, where an old prophet meets a younger prophet. The older prophet says, "I am a prophet just like you," and later convinces the younger to go home with him and thus disobey a direct order from God. Listening to the older prophet cost the younger prophet his life. *The problem here is that the older prophet used his title as a means of manipulation for personal benefit, an issue we too often see today.*

Jesus says something enlightening about prophets in Luke 7:28. "For I say to you, among those born of women *there is not a greater prophet than John the Baptist*; but he who is least in the kingdom of god is greater than he." Let's ponder this for a moment. Did Jesus say John was a prophet? Yes he did. Jesus also said he was the *greatest* prophet ever born. However, when the Levites and priest pressed John to define himself in John 1:19-23, his answer did not satisfy them. Actually, it blows my mind.

Now this is John's testimony, given when the Jews sent priests and Levites from Jerusalem to inquire, "Who are you?" He confessed and did not deny, "I am not the Christ." And they asked him, "What then? Are you Elijah?" He said, "I am not." *"Are you the prophet?"*

And he answered, "No." Then they said to him, "Who are you, that we may give an answer to those who sent us? What do you say about yourself?" What a profound statement comes next: *"I am 'the voice of one crying in the wilderness: 'make straight the way of the lord," As the prophet Isaiah said."*

Okay, out of the mouth of Jesus, we see that John has just received the highest endorsement from the one who gave the office of prophets to the church.

However, John was so focused *on his own ministry beginning to disappear to make way for the Messiah,* that he dared not boast in the title to the religious elite, and detract the focus from Jesus, where it belonged.

If you're one of my Pentecostal friends, please don't raise a stone for me just yet.

I fully believe in the five-fold ministry of Ephesians chapter 4, and that all of the gifts of the Spirit are still in operation. Furthermore, God has often chosen to operate his prophetic anointing through our ministry. However, I personally like to view these Ephesians' "offices" more on the lines of *functions*, not *titles*. Functions build up the church, titles build up personalities. I also believe that our focus at times has skewed away from the heart of Christ and the spirit of John the Baptist. I once heard Lou Giglio say, "John the Baptist had a passion for a vanishing ministry." This is an uncommon passion to put it mildly.

There is a title in the Kingdom of God that is far greater than Apostle, Prophet, Prophetess, Pastor, Teacher, or Evangelist. Jesus was addressing the twelve foundational Apostles when he made this statement… "And the greatest among you shall be your *servant*." A great servant may not ever draw a crowd, but my bet is that he or she will know how to take care of one.

It is interesting to note that this infatuation with power and position in the church is nothing new. It was evident in some of the early disciples as found in Luke 10:17-20.

The seventy returned with joy and said, "Lord, even the demons submit to us in your name."

He replied, "I saw Satan fall like lightening from heaven.

I have given you authority to trample on snakes and scorpions and to overcome all the power of the enemy; nothing will harm you. However, do not rejoice that the spirits submit to you, but rejoice that *your names are written in heaven*." (NIV)

When the seventy returned from ministering, they were astounded by the power of the Gospel. The sick were healed, miracles were happening, and demons were being evicted.

Wouldn't you be filled with awe as well? After their debriefing to Jesus, you would think that he would immediately chime in to their excitement. He does not.

After observing what was really going on in their hearts, Jesus is curt and somewhat reprimanding in telling them not to rejoice because of all the victories they had witnessed, but only rejoice in the fact that their *names were written in heaven*. Upon studying his words to the disciples, I believe that what Jesus *might* have implied was this: *Do not rejoice at the byproduct of relationship, just rejoice in the fact that the relationship exists.*

This mentality of the disciples is still alive and well, and defines too much of modern church doctrine and conference agendas. An inordinate amount of teaching focuses on the privileges that flow from relationship with God. Sadly, it often ignores the blessing that sonship is just available, and the opportunity to explore the unfathomable depths of who our Father is!

If not careful, this over emphasis on the *byproducts* can pervert our worship into a performance-based servanthood. We see this in the story of Martha and Mary. Martha was doing what she was gifted to do, cook and prepare meals as if it were a work of art. The kitchen was Martha's sweet spot, and she was working hard to create a beautiful setting and meal for

Jesus and the disciples. When Jesus admonished her, in a gentle way to adjust her priorities, he was not telling her to stop being Martha, but simply to recognize when to choose the "better thing." Oh that we would learn when to stop doing and simply be, when we too would just choose the better thing and to sit at the feet of Jesus and receive his love and truth.

Again, soapbox over for now.

Let's revisit a scripture that's at the beginning of this chapter. If you examine it with a discerning heart, you may find *the* single most liberating truth for God's servants and the path to Kingdom greatness.

Jesus knew that the Father had put all things under his power,

and that he had come from God and was returning to God,

so he got up from the meal, took off his outer clothing and

wrapped a towel around his waist. After that he poured water

into a basin and began to wash his disciples' feet, drying them

with the towel that was wrapped around him.

(John 13:3-5 NIV)

The story tells us about the intimate Passover meal right before Jesus' death. His time with the disciples was ending.

They had seen him minister in many different situations, but he was about to *stun* them as he proceeded to wash their feet.

Foot washing in that day was about as low on the social, much less ministry totem pole as you could go. Usually this job was reserved for slaves, and let me explain why. Roads were unpaved. Animals had droppings. Rains came. Mud and other *stuff* would ooze between toes...you get the picture.

Anyway, Jesus moves into position to wash the disciples' feet, as he is about to demonstrate the way and the attitude that should characterize their ministry from this point forward. Jesus' actions so offended Peter, that he almost stopped his rabbi before he could begin. **However, what is pertinent here, what is the linchpin of this chapter, is not just *what Jesus did*, but even more, the *preamble to what he did*.** Let's take a look at verse three.

> ...Jesus, knowing that the Father had given all things into his hands, and that *He had come from God* and *was going to God*...

Here, we observe God the Son, who had no need to submit to servitude but did so anyway. In addition, the Holy Spirit gives us a glimpse into Jesus' pedigree and maybe even more important, *his eternal frame of reference*. Child of God, please understand this, Jesus knew exactly who he was.

Jesus was the one who by and through him all things are made. He was the one that upholds everything by the very power of his word. He made the dirty roads. He created the animals that would trudge over them and their digestive tracts that would produce droppings. He caused the rain to fall that would ultimately soil the feet of the disciples, which he also created. Friend, Jesus knew who he was, where he came from, and where he was going. He did not mind getting his hands a little dirty.

If we will recall, he had done it once before back on a playground called creation. Let me just say before I go any further, how much I love and need a savior and King who *still* stoops to wash what is filthy.

Know this; When Jesus bent down to begin his task, those twelve men really had no clue of the Divine Dignitary that was cleaning dirt and dung off their feet...*but he knew*. They believed, but could in no way fully comprehend the fact that Jesus was on loan to earth, and that his eternal throne sat right beside Yahweh's...*but he did*.

Jesus knew. He created all things and would soon ascend and return to his rightful place beside his Father. The crux of this passage and the take away is this:

Jesus' had no identity crisis! His self-worth was not wrapped up in what *he was doing* in the moment. His identity was forever connected to *who he was* in the Father!

My question to you is direct and hopefully poignant. Are you identified by what you do, or is your existence rooted in who Heaven declares you are? This is the liberating question and key that empowers servanthood.

If you know your identity, you can do anything, and never be afraid of what *they* will say. You will never fear being overlooked, underpaid, under applauded, or *under anointed*. You will never have to shout who you are, tout what you have done, tell how much you are worth, or promote your agenda. Your identity is secure and like Jesus, you have *an eternal frame of reference that is wrapped up in sonship*.

Oh, there are so many in the Body of Christ that have not connected with the power of this truth and how to live it out.

I have two friends, Tony and Christy Seepe, who started a ministry called "Improve Your Serve." (www.improveyourserve.com) I have never met anyone who epitomizes the heart of Christ-like character and servanthood more than these two people. Their whole ministry focus is to come under the mission of other ministries they support. In whatever venue they serve, their heart's desire is to handle the mundane, behind the scenes details that would impede advancing the gospel. Their hearts and spirits are rare indeed!

One of my favorite historical examples of this is kind of servanthood is from Steve Brown's book, *Jumping Hurdles, Hitting Glitches, Overcoming Setbacks*. Steve tells a story that takes place during The American Revolution, when a man in civilian clothes rode past a group of soldiers repairing a small defensive barrier. "Their leader was shouting instructions at them but making no other attempt to help them. Asked why by the rider, the leader said with great dignity, 'Sir, I'm a corporal!' The stranger apologized, dismounted, and proceeded to help the exhausted soldiers. The job done, he turned to the corporal and said, 'If you need some more help, son, call me.' With that, the Commander-in-chief, George Washington, remounted his horse and rode on."[10]

Obviously Washington knew who he was; and history, (without his input), has lauded his greatness. Too many precious children of God have not embraced this kind of spirit. They ascribe self-appointed titles and pursue endless degrees, attaching these to their names with one goal, a longing to fill the void of affirmation that only comes from joyful service to the Master.

I have seen them corral a Holy Ghost *posse* to surround their every move, supposedly to *protect their anointing*, but in truth, to constantly fill their vacuum of self worth. They are beyond the thought of getting too close to others, much less serving them in obscurity, as *servant* sounds so beneath Apostle, Prophet, Pastor, Teacher, and Evangelist.

However, again, when all that exists will come to its end, *the commendation* we hope our Father will bestow is this: "… Well done thou good and faithful servant!"

Not long ago, I was watching one of the nature channels on television. They were filming a pride of lions on the grasslands of the Serengeti. As the lions stirred from their nap, I watched a huge male shake himself and step out of the tall grass into view by the other animals. The camera panned to zebras, antelopes, and other grazers. For a few moments I watched in awe, riveted by him. Then suddenly, all the animals went on high alert as they sensed the king of the jungle's presence. It was then I felt the Holy Spirit speak to me saying, "Jon, they all know he is there, *though he hasn't made a sound*...The power of his presence is enough."

Then the Spirit then spoke something else to my heart that I will never forget. "The lion knows who he is. Though he has not announced his presence, he understands the effect of its power. A true servant, a true child of God, who knows who he or she is, can do anything I ask them to do; the power of my presence in them is enough."

The Lord then whispered these words that resounded like a megaphone in my spirit:

Lions don't have to roar.

Do you know who you are? Are you safe enough in your identity to wash feet, pass out church bulletins, scrub toilets, or change dirty diapers in the nursery? Can you bless and rejoice with others when they advance in the kingdom, but the light of recognition has not shined your way? On the other hand, do you have to roar about your anointing, your connections, your accomplishments or even your blessings to secure your identity?

It may not be a ministry or church thing at all for you. Your proving ground may be the workplace. Are you secure enough in him, that when *they* receive the promotion, *they* make the big sell, or *they* receive the invitation to the important meeting, that you can continue to serve humbly in obscurity with excellence as in Acts Chapter 6? God does desire to promote and bless you; however, He is too loving to do that before *due season.* When is that you might ask? When he will get the most glory and it will be for your most good.

For the last few years I've been ministering to corporate America, to businessmen and women who—like you and me—have been affected by the devastating blows to our economy. People have faced unprecedented financial difficulties and setbacks as the fierce winds of adversity have blown away hopes and dreams seemingly in an instant.

Well, in offering these men and women hope, that God will use their difficulties for their good and his glory, I often quote Isaiah 49:2:

"He made my mouth like a sharpened sword, in the shadow of his hand he hid me; he made me into a polished arrow and concealed me in his quiver."

What does God plan to do with this polished arrow, keep it hidden forever? No, he sends it forth to proclaim his truth, to accomplish his work. And what we perceive as setbacks—failures and flops—are the very things God will use to prepare us for our destiny. I've done a bit of study on archery, and when an archer is going to release an arrow, he pulls it in the *opposite direction* of where it was forged to go.

Just think, what we may perceive as a setback—having to work in the Kingdom or elsewhere in obscurity, in the mundane,—may very well be the Father adding torque to the arrow of your destiny. It could be that right now he is positioning you, making you ready for release at precisely the right time. And know this: the Divine Archer always releases his polished arrow when the winds are just right to carry it as far as it needs to go. In other words, set backs are set ups...for a comeback!

If you really want to know what Jesus thinks about *greatness*, I encourage you to visit the story found in Mark 10:35-45. James and John were jockeying for position in Heaven's Kingdom. They ask Jesus to let them sit on his right and left hand in his Heavenly realm. Jesus' response is sobering. In essence he says to them; if you want to reign with me, you will have to die with me, and only the Father has the right to choose those eternal places of honor. In this passage Jesus addresses promotion or greatness in scripture for the last time.

And whoever of you desires to be first shall be slave of all. For even the Son of Man did not come to be served, but to serve, and to give his life a ransom for many."
(Mark 10:44-45)

Only one training camp leads to greatness in our Father's Kingdom. It is the often unheralded and unseen school of servanthood. Know this: Though everyone has a membership, not enough of God's children want to complete the necessary training; however, Apollo Creed's gymnasium is still open.

Chapter 7

Divine Delivery

And Moses went up to God, and the LORD called to him from the mountain, saying, "Thus you shall say to the house of Jacob, and tell the children of Israel: You have seen what I did to the Egyptians, and how I bore you on eagles' wings *and brought you to Myself.*

(Exodus 19:3-4)

Now all the people witnessed the thunderings, the lightning flashes, the sound of the trumpet, and the mountain smoking; and when the people saw it, they trembled and stood afar off. Then they said to Moses, "You speak with us, and we will hear; *but let not God speak with us, lest we die."*

(Exodus 20:18-19)

But as it is written: "Eye has not seen, nor ear heard, Nor have entered into the heart of man The things which God has prepared for those who love Him." *But God has revealed them to us through his Spirit.* For the Spirit searches all things, yes, the deep things of God. For what man knows the things of a man except the spirit of the man which is in him? Even so no one knows the things of God except the Spirit of God. *Now we have received, not the spirit of the world, but the Spirit who is from God, that we might know the things that have been freely given to us by God.*

(1 Corinthians 2:9-12)

E very time I have heard a sermon on this last passage of scripture, it centered on Heaven and sorta' sounded like this: *"Bless God - **hah**... one day when we all get to heaven - **hah**, we'll finally get to see what eye hath not seen, nor ear hath heard - **hah**. I can't wait to get my mansion, now how 'bout you! – **hah**."*

Okay, so I am just poking a little fun here at my Pentecostal heritage, ***hah***.

Seriously, I do not mean to be cynical, and you could certainly apply this scripture broadly in that context, but the above interpretation is not the aim of Paul's exhortation. Here, Paul is offering us a key to Kingdom living and a privilege of sonship. He is saying that God has some deep and hidden plans for his children.

Paul further informs us that these plans are so far beyond our natural cognition, that we can only download them via Divine revelation from Spirit to spirit. The question is how do we get there, how can we access them?

Well first, we must understand that our Father is the quintessential daydreamer. He invented the concept. Think of it. I wonder if eons ago, maybe Father God saw a sparkle in Jesus' eyes, and then suddenly he conceived the cosmos! I do know this. He has unfathomable and inexhaustible creativity and power. The instant he speaks, what he has envisioned is produced. He truly is the *celestial imaginer* who dreams and acts in holy grandiose; furthermore, we were created to be like him!

The wonderful thing is that God does not dream for naught. He really, really desires that we discover his imaginings. Did you know that he thinks about you far more than you could ever comprehend? David knew this as he wrote Psalm 139. "How precious to me are your thoughts, O God! How vast is the sum of them. Were I to count them; *they would outnumber the grains of sand*. (17-18)

How about a number totaling around 2000 billion, billion thoughts, give or take a few hundred million. That is the estimated number of grains of sand on the earth right now according to Glen Mackie, Professor of Astrophysics and Supercomputing at the Swinburne University of Technology in Australia.[11] (I can truly say I never knew such a profession existed.)

Okay, just for fun, I did some arithmetic myself. I thought it would be cool to multiply Dr. Mackie's number, by the roughly six billion people on the earth right now.

Are you ready? In addition to all the other routine things on his "to do" list, God is thinking at least *12 decillion*, or 12,000 ,000,000,000,000,000,000,000,000,000 thoughts at any given moment!

That number hurts my mind and eyes; however, it does underscore a point that we need to get. The Psalmist words and Dr. Mackie's calculations reinforce that indeed our Father is a big thinker to put it mildly. What is on his mind is even more amazing. You, yes you are my friend. He is thinking about you, *apparently quite often*.

If what David said is accurate, and we know it is, then how can we possibly connect with just a few of God's thoughts towards us? What causes him to want to divulge his clandestine plans that Paul declares he has for his children? Well first, we have to believe that he truly desires to reveal them.

One of my favorite passages of scripture is Daniel Chapter 2 where King Nebuchadnezzar has just sentenced young Belteshazzzar, (Daniel's Babylonian name), to death. Daniel doesn't fear but answers in confidence, "Praise be to the name of God for ever and ever; wisdom and power are his. He changes time and seasons; he sets up kings and deposes them. He gives wisdom to the wise and knowledge to the discerning. *He reveals deep and hidden things; he knows what lies in darkness and light dwells with him."*

Daniel informs us that God not only knows the deep and the secret things, but that he reveals them. Wow! How about that? The greatest secrets in the universe are now accessible, and you have the inside track to discover them first. In the paradigm of us as God's kids, this makes perfect sense. Being a daddy myself, I love to whisper secrets to my children that no one else gets to hear.

Now, if this sounds like a deal you want in on, let me give you a head start. There is only one way to connect with God and that is through intimacy. Intimacy with the Father is what we need most, yet often experience least. I think that intimacy can be described in its simplest form, as *deep and reciprocal, knowledge, fellowship, and love.*

Intimacy takes effort. It flows out of two postures - humility and vulnerability. If you are married, you probably understand. I embraced both of these when I fell in love with Lisa. First, I had to humble myself and admit that I desperately needed her. No more *the player, or "Cat Daddy"*, as my frat brothers used to call me.

The first time Lisa and I went out; we ended up talking for 5 hours. I had never connected with anyone on so many levels as I did with her. Not only was she absolutely beautiful, but we had and still have an amazing ease in communicating and understanding one another. Also, she is the only person I ever dated who consistently made me laugh, and still does today.

I realized life would be empty if I lost her presence. After this epiphany, I became *vulnerable*. Not only do I need you Lisa, but I am revealing myself to you. Here are my *warts*, my idiosyncrasies, my brokenness and my baggage. Did she still want me? Thank God she did.

I understand that intimacy for many of us, especially men, does not come easy. If you have difficulty with it, you are not unlike roughly three million Hebrews in the Old Testament. In Exodus 19 and 20, we see God's first visitation with the children of Israel in the wilderness. This is post-Egypt and post-Red Sea. God tells Moses to prepare the people, as he wants to come down and have a *fireside chat*.

During Franklin Roosevelt's term as president back in the 30's, he began a series of radio broadcasts to the American people reassuring them the nation was going to recover from the depression. In those "fireside chats," he spoke to them from the White House as they tuned in from their living rooms, sharing his hopes and plans for the country. The talks often began with *"Good evening, friend."* In those days he urged listeners to have faith in the banks.

God wanted to have a fireside chat of his own with Israel. His just happened to include setting an entire mountain top ablaze, along with a few earthquakes and lighting bolts, and he urged his listeners to have faith in Yahweh, the Great I Am. *"I am the Lord your God who brought you out of Egypt…you shall have no other gods before me."* What really happened at Sinai in this story—I think—was that the earth was smart enough to quake, and lightening wise enough to strike when their creator dropped by.

I have to say it's so odd to me that humanity, the zenith of Genesis, still gets antsy about expressive worship; however, the rest of creation readily knows how to applaud its maker.

Moving on with this story, we see an interaction between the people and their God that is not *too* uncommon today. God steps down from Heaven to connect with his children; but this time, he becomes *vulnerable* to the Israelites. He is vulnerable in the sense that Israel encounters a new revelation of Yahweh.

God tells Moses that in the same personal way he had been communicating with this former Egyptian prince turned shepherd, he desired to fellowship with the Israelites. In light of all God had done on their behalf, the response from the people was a bit unexpected.

When God's vulnerability discloses a side unknown to them, they reject him and his desire for their fellowship. This following passage is very revealing: "Now all the people witnessed the thunderings, the lightning flashes, the sound of the trumpet, and the mountain smoking; and when the people saw it, they trembled and stood afar off. Then they said to Moses, "You speak with us, and we will hear; **but let not God speak with us, lest we die**." (Exodus 20:18-19)

It was natural for them to rejoice when *that* God invaded Egypt, the thundering, lightening flashing God, who decimated a nation. They could go out singing his praises as they exited Egypt, adorned in the fine linen and gold of their former taskmasters. They could sing halleluiah as the Red Sea became a watery burial ground for Pharaoh and his soldiers. However, when *that* God of all the miracles discloses that he is also *this* God of Mount Sinai, it is too much for the Israelites to handle. If you examine verses 20 and 21 of this passage, you see what is *really going on*.

Moses told them not to be afraid, that God had not come to test them, but to show them his great power and authority, "so the fear of God will be with you to keep you from sinning." When God reveals himself to us in this type of intimate way, we also become keenly aware of how holy he is and how unholy we are. We differ from him as much as darkness does to light. Moreover, as Moses said, his *fear* accompanies him. This fear is not the kind that makes you run away, but the kind that makes you look deep within to your true self. It is better described as an intense holy awe that accompanies his presence.

During Yom Kipper, it is traditional for Jews to read and meditate on Scripture for the "days of awe." They read Exodus 20 along with Psalm 145 about exalting, praising, extolling his name. *"One generation will commend your works to another; they will tell of your mighty acts. They will speak of the glorious splendor of your majesty…They will tell of the power of your awesome works…"*(Psalm 145:4-6) They read and meditate on the Ten Commandments, and seek reconciliation and forgiveness. Something amazing happens when we pray these words. *You, alone my Lord are holy. Purify my soul, my mind and heart. Renew me. Implant your awe into my being.*

Such divine consciousness always reveals the darkness in our hearts and magnifies its unresolved sin issues. This heightened sense of just how holy God is will keep us spiritually alert. Moses alluded to this when he said that if the Israelites would welcome his presence, this fear — this holy awe — would keep them from sinning. However, this was *too* much for the children of Israel to process.

Egypt's gods never came down and manifested their awesome power. Isis, Re, Ammut, Osiris and the others, never once spoke their mind. They certainly never engaged individuals for mere fellowship.

Even in light of their resistance, in this 20th passage of Exodus, Yahweh speaks the great desire of his heart. He wants three million people with a heart like Moses'. He wants to get to know each and everyone of them intimately.

Observe God's heart in the following verses:

"Now therefore, if you will indeed obey My voice and keep My covenant, *then **you shall be a special treasure to Me above all people***; for all the earth is Mine. **And you shall be to Me a kingdom of priests and a holy nation.** These are the words which you shall speak to the children of Israel." (Exodus 19:5-6) God reveals that he has called the Israelites out of slavery to be his very own special treasure, a new class of priestly royalty, but they did not get it. It went over their heads.

Let me stop here and segue for a moment to illuminate a key principle of how God works, a principle that is hidden in this Exodus passage. Romans 4:17 sheds further light on it.

When the Apostle Paul explained the relationship between God and Abraham, (and the amazing faith Abraham had), he said that God's nature gives life to the dead and calls those things *which do not exist* as though they *did*. (Romans 4:17-18)

As with Abraham, God beholds all his children with this same prophetic prospective. This includes you, me and the Israelites. Our Father sees us through the future lens of what he knows we are to become, not through the limitations of our present condition or geographic location. God speaks of us in this *future-present* tense, because in his mind *we are as he sees us*.

When I was running as hard as I could from God, while I was sinning as bad as I was in my teens and twenties, God had already decided that I would be a voice to preach his gospel. When I hated the thought of ever ministering in a pulpit and scoffed at those who saw his calling on my life, God saw me boldly preaching his word to 65,000 Nigerians at a crusade, just as I did in March of 2010. Therefore, when God addresses the Israelites as *kings* and *priests here in Exodus*; we see a consistent trait of the Father throughout scripture. *He always speaks prophetically to the destiny imbedded within us.*

Abram becomes Abraham, the father of many nations. Barren Sarai becomes Sarah, the queen of mothers. Manipulative Jacob is renamed Israel, the Prince of God and the apple of his eye. Joseph the prisoner is Joseph the prime minister. Moses the stutterer becomes Moses the deliverer. Gideon the coward is soon Gideon the conqueror. Simon the unstable is Peter the Rock; and so on it goes throughout God's word.

It bolsters my heart to know that when I perceived myself as Jon the misfit, Jon the abused, and Jon the damaged goods, that my Father God saw me as Jon his minister, Jon his champion, but most of all, Jon his beloved son in whom he was and is well-pleased! In all of these instances, God speaks from the realm of the Spirit down into the realm of the natural, even if the natural is in blatant disagreement with what he is saying.

My favorite example of Romans 4:17 in action is found in the book of Exodus, chapters 32 and then chapter 28. When Moses didn't come down from the mountain right away, the people wonder what has become of him. They beg his brother

Aaron to make them a symbol, something familiar they could see and worship.

So Aaron tells them, "Break off the golden earrings which are in the ears of your wives, your sons, and your daughters, and bring them to me." From all this gold, he molds an idol in the shape of a calf, and the people respond, "This is your god, O Israel, that brought you out of the land of Egypt!" (Exodus 32:2-5)

All the while Moses is up on Mount Sinai in chapter 28, receiving instructions about governing and leading the Israelites. The Israelites, growing impatient on hearing from God, take matters into their own hands and appoint Aaron as their new leader and pagan priest.

We now know the rest of the story, as Aaron apparently forgets God and his brother, and leads over three million people into idolatry and hedonism. Now typically, we stop and reflect on Aaron's and Israel disobedience as the central take away from this story and move on. However, what I want you to see — in light of Romans 4:17 — is what *God is saying about Aaron* over in Exodus 28, as Aaron is putting the finishing touches on that golden calf in Exodus 32.

"Now take Aaron your brother, and his sons with him, from among the children of Israel, that he may minister to Me as priest, Aaron and Aaron's sons: Nadab, Abihu, Eleazar, and Ithamar. 2 And you shall make holy garments for Aaron your brother, for glory and for beauty. 3 So you shall speak to all who are gifted artisans, whom I have filled with the spirit of wisdom, that they may make Aaron's garments, to consecrate him, that he may minister to Me as priest. And these are the garments that they shall make: a breastplate, an ephod, a robe, a skillfully woven tunic, a turban, and a sash.

So they shall make holy garments for Aaron your brother and his sons, that he may minister to Me as priest. (Exodus 28:1-4)

Yaaay God! This has to be one of the coolest things I have ever seen in scripture! While our boy Aaron is leading three million people in an idolatrous debauchery, Father God is up on the mountain calling Aaron his first high priest! Not just a priest, but also the founding head of all the Levitical Priesthood! He and his family line are the ones that God is entrusting to get the job done...golden earrings and all.

What we have to understand here is that God is always speaking from a higher vantage point of revelation about the prophetic destiny that is in his kids, and how he envisions our legacy on the earth. It doesn't matter how far away we feel we are or have wandered from his plans for us. Our Father's dreams and hopes for us *will* happen, in spite of our past or present performance, or lack thereof. Aaron certainly had is low points, but God still used him.

So, back to his dealings with Israel, we see God's first act of communication with these disenfranchised pyramid builders was to rename them "kings and priests." What makes this so ironic is that this former slave caste of Egypt had only served cruel Pharaohs and endured four-hundred years of pagan worship. However, God speaks to the future as if it were present. He weaves in and out through past, present and future, as they are all the same to him, calling us to embrace what we really are, yet have not seen manifest. Our Father saw Israel as his special nation of royal priests; sadly, they never were able to embrace their calling.

Not only did they not live up to God's expectations, the Israelites quickly decided that *this* God was fine if he would keep his mouth shut. Don't we do that sometimes? We want to be in the family of God, take part in all the social events, volunteer our time, give our money, and we don't mind a little nudging here and there, *but our flesh cringes at the thought of bold directives from him*. For example, in Luke 18, we find the story of the rich young ruler that Jesus instructed to go and sell what he had to give to the poor, and then come an follow Jesus.

This story shows how true discipleship is often costly, but even more, by not obeying the Lord, this young ruler lost the opportunity to possibly become the thirteenth disciple.

In essence, the Israelites told Moses to be their ears and eyes to this God of Sinai, *but our hearts are off limits.* How often do we take the same posture as the children of Israel? We encourage our pastor to get close to God, applaud his sermons on transformation and contribute to his costs for attending seminars and retreats that grow him as a spiritual leader.

We support the elders and deacons in their efforts to grow and draw near to God, but we're not sure we want to make such a serious commitment ourselves. Too often, we men, and I include myself, let our wives take the lead in spiritual matters at church and home. Sometimes it's out of necessarily, as we men are often away from home trying to provide for our families. I remember how Lisa had to forge a passion for God in our kids as I traipsed from city to city during my tenure in corporate America.

The truth is, that women involuntarily assume the role of spiritual leader in the home due to the spiritual laziness of their spouses. Sometimes it's an attitude of: *Let God speak with anyone other than me. I'm busy being the provider.* The Israelites, even in their stubbornness, spoke a profound truth in

Exodus 20:19, but were probably not aware of it at the time. "…
Let not God speak to us… lest we *die"*

The closer we draw to God, something in us called our flesh
or our carnality must *die*. The true message of intimacy with
him again resounds in the words of John the Baptist. "He must
increase and I must decrease." No one really wants to hear this,
but death to self is the only doorway to intimacy with God.
Why would God have it that way? Because no one clothed
in flesh has a right to live in the all-consuming purity and fire
of his glory. I struggled dying to myself. Ever since I decided
to be the *Terminator* at age eight, I'd been running my own
life, making things happen. I had no idea what surrender really
meant. We'll address this dying to self a little more in the next
chapter.

How dismal if it ended there, his glory demanding our
death.

As I noted before, the beautiful fact is when God is in the
picture, nothing ever dies in his presence without a resurrection. He is the resurrection and the life. It is the power of his
resurrection operating in our spirit man, which allows us to
hear his voice, his thoughts and dreams for us.

Not long ago I asked God to show me just what happens
when we truly draw near to him and he draws near to us. How

do we really access those wonderful things, "that our eyes have not seen nor our ears have heard," things Paul assures are waiting for us.

I felt the Lord say that there are clear correlations between birthing a child in the natural, and bringing forth something new that is spiritual.

For a baby to be delivered into this world, at least these seven things will occur.

1. Nakedness
2. Intimacy
3. Impregnation
4. Morning sickness
5. Gestation
6. Travail
7. Birth

There are spiritual correlations to these:

1. Nakedness – If we are to go anywhere with God, we must be real with nothing hidden. His holiness demands that we see ourselves as we are without the covering of false faces, agendas, or desires. It is interesting that our automatic response to nakedness cover ourselves! Adam immediately felt a need to cover himself as soon as his sin was exposed. God cannot work with covered flesh. David said in Psalm 51:6 "Behold, you desire truth in the inward parts, and in the hidden part you will make me to know wisdom." When we get real, God does his best work in us.

2. ***Intimacy*** – This is the place of humility and vulnerability, where we respond to him in worship and total submission. We listen for his voice as the deer pants for the water. We yearn for his presence, forsaking all others. We quickly realize that he alone is our source and resource.

    We have been created for his pleasure and nothing more; furthermore, we know that we can do nothing without him nor would we want to. This is why we exist.

3. ***Impregnation*** – When intimacy is flowing unencumbered, we are then in position to hear his heartbeat. It is then that our spirits will be seeded with God-given dreams and God designed plans.

    Here the imperishable seed of his *rhema* or word is spoken in us and we get revelation of what he desires and has planned for us. It is where the mysteries of Jeremiah 29:11 begin to unveil.

4. **Mourning sickness** – In the spirit, it is not *morning* sickness but *mourning* sickness. This is the place where we become nauseated with the spiritual condition of our existence. It is where we desperately cry out for a new manifestation of God's glory, where we beg for nothing but what he says we will be. It's here that we lament the true state of our wretchedness without him. It's what I cried out that day, *change me*. It must be God's message through the prophet Joel: *"Turn to me with all your heart, with fasting, with weeping, and with mourning."*

5. *Gestation* – As it is in the natural, this is the place for preparation and order, the place of adjustments. Any mother can attest to the fact that as a child develops in the womb, things that used to fit no longer do. In the spiritual, this is where we adapt to accommodate God-sized directives and mandates. Old thought patterns and paradigms are shattered here. Often, this is the place where God directs us to make changes in relationships.

Here we are called evaluate allegiances and to connect with like-minded believers who are God seekers as well. This is where we "Prepare ye the way of The Lord."

6. ***Travail*** – Once gestation has occurred, we enter a season where our prayers cry out for heaven's dreams to manifest on earth. In travail, we are about to experience the blessed event. Distractions are gone, focus becomes laser sharp. This is where we get in agreement with what God desires. We agree that we want nothing less than his Kingdom come, his will be done. It is this crucible where the vision lives or dies, where all resources and energy center on bringing into fruition what God has ordained.

7. ***Birth*** – His Kingdom comes at last. We move from glory to glory. His will is done.

In Paul's first letter to the Corinthians, Chapter two highlights this place of birthing; in God's secret wisdom, destined for our glory before time began. "No mind has conceived what God has prepared for those who love him." (v. 9) Like Israel, God calls us out of a place of slavery to spiritual sonship. The Israelites never really figured this out, but God delivered them from slaves in Egypt *just to be with him*. In Exodus 19:4 God tells Moses to tell his people what he did for them in Egypt, how he rescued them from slavery, *"how I carried you on eagles' wings and brought you to myself."*

God brought them out of bondage, not so he could make them a mighty nation nor take them on a journey into Canaan. No, he delivered them to demonstrate his desire for their fellowship and love. He wanted intimacy.

How God's heart must have been broken as he showed himself to them daily; at dawn, a pillar of cloud for them to follow, and at dusk, a pillar of fire to illuminate their way through the night. They had no desire to know him as anything more than a guide. *Only Moses loved him back.* Only Moses sought him out. What an incomprehensible and sad thought. Israel had the unprecedented privilege to get to know Yahweh personally. They squandered forty years—or 14,600 days, 350,400 minutes—and ignored a heart longing to commune with them.

Even though the thought of communicating with God is hugely intimidating, we have to believe that intimacy with us is his primary goal, his first idea. He wants to know us as well.

Hollywood came out with a movie called, *"He's Not that Into You,"* which follows the lives of a dozen or so characters in and out of the dating scene. It highlights the behavior of insincere men and the games they play with women until they find "the one." Let me promise you of something right now...

God never plays games with our hearts and I can assure you my friend, God *is* just that *in to you*!

Like the Children of Israel, we are still his special treasure that he has delivered from the chains of the bondage of sin, for one sole reason—fellowship. I believe his desire for the Israelites stems all the way back to the third book of Genesis, which alludes that God walked with man in the cool of the evening.

I like to think that Adam and Eve had a 5 pm appointment with their Father every day. I imagine it was about 70 degrees with a soft breeze blowing and zero humidity. There in Eden, God and his children would walk, talk, and laugh together; a unique time where his children discovered the amazing mysteries of who their father was and all had planned for them. Again, God thought of fellowship first. God wanted fellowship. God initiated fellowship.

The staggering truth is that in light of all of my faults and frailty, God still wants to hear my voice. Sometimes this fact blows me away. And he still wants to hear your voice. He still yearns to pick up with us where he left off with his first children in Eden, and reveal his glorious hidden mysteries he has for your life! I wonder if the story of redemption can be wrapped up like this; the big hand on God's watch is eternally set at twelve, and the little hand is still on the five.

What dreams do you ponder? Have you connected with his dreams, his plans, and his heart for you? I recall an adage that says if you want to go where you've never been, you have to do what you've never done. What are you willing to do to experience God in a way that you have never been able to before? Are you game to become impregnated with destiny? I assure you he is waiting on your embrace. Jeremiah told us that his hopes and plans for us are good. David said our Lord daydreams about you a lot.

God loves working with dreamers and delivering what he inspires! Consider the company of those who dared to envision what their eyes could not see and what their ears had not heard:

Abraham had a dream about a son.   God delivered.
Joseph had a dream about wheat that curtsied.   God delivered
Ruth had a dream about a Boaz.   God delivered.
Moses had a dream about freedom.   God delivered.
Hannah had a dream about a baby.   God delivered.
David had a dream about a kingdom.   God delivered.
Solomon had a dream about a temple.   God delivered.
Zerubbabel had a dream about restoration.   God delivered.
Esther had a dream about justice.   God delivered.
God had a dream about redemption.   *Jesus* delivered.

If you glean anything here, please let it be this: Know your Father! Fellowship with your Father! Dream with your Father! As you dream with God, he will progressively reveal his will, line upon line, precept upon precept, as the tapestry of your life unfolds. Our father is the divine playwright who has each scene of our lives uniquely crafted to bring him glory.

Shakespeare in *"As You Like It,"* penned that all the world's a stage, and each man and women are merely players. In our lifetime we play many parts; so true, and sometimes we play parts never written for us. But if we follow the dreams God plants in our hearts from the script he has written for us, we'll naturally play the role on the stage of life that nobody else is born to play.

Had I not heeded God's call on my life, I likely would be stuck in a cubicle or office in some corporate entity, wondering what if? Randall Weeks, a friend of mine, once said: *God forbid that you should walk across the stage of life, and to never have said your lines.*

I say, find your script!

Chapter 8

Dead Men, Peter Pan and
The Great Vaccine

What shall we say, then? Shall we go on sinning so that grace

may increase? By no means! We died to sin;

how can we live in it any longer?

(Romans 6:1-3 NIV)

Therefore, since we are receiving a kingdom which cannot

be shaken, let us have grace, by which we may serve God

acceptably with reverence and Godly fear for

our God is a consuming fire.

(Hebrews 12:28-29)

For certain men whose condemnation was written about long

ago have secretly slipped in among you. They are Godless men,

who change the grace of our God into a license for immorality,

and deny Jesus Christ our only sovereign and Lord.

(Jude 4:4)

He who overcomes shall inherit all things, and I will be his

God and he shall be My *son*.

(Revelation 21:7)

G od has blessed us with three amazing children, all teenagers now. Elliott, Barrett, and Kelsey are the best, and
what's more incredible, *they have never disobeyed*. Now if by
chance you believe that, may I also interest you in some resort
land on the coast of Colorado?

According to Scripture, especially Galatians 5:19-21, we
are hard-wired for disobedience. We are born with a rebellious
spirit. You don't have to observe any group of toddlers in day-
care for more than a few minutes, to realize that the Adamic
nature of self-will is alive and well, and sometimes kicking...
right in the shin!

We expect disobedience from our kids, and we often laugh
at their pouts and their pudgy little hands on the hips, the way
they scowl and blurt, "No!" However, stubbornness is not so

cute in God's adult children. I have come to realize that my sin nature is a whole lot like Peter Pan.

Peter was a good enough kid, but he had one major unresolved issue – he flatly refused to grow up and mature. My carnal nature is the same way. God has only one remedy for this. Francois Fineberg, a brilliant teacher and covenant brother of mine, once told me that when you really think about it, Satan and God actually have the same agenda for my life - *to destroy my flesh*. One wants me to die in damnation, the other, to die and live again in abundant life.

This second choice though obvious, is impossible to experience without the power of God living through this earthen vessel. The same is true for you. Many of us would like to cut this part out of the school of sonship. It is *the* most difficult lesson to learn and the term is quite lengthy. School ends at the bell of your last breath.

The Apostle Paul knew about this struggle we all face. In the final chapter of his life, he exhorts young Timothy, who is at the height of his own ministry. Paul says, *I have fought the good fight, I have finished the race, I have kept the faith*. (2 Timothy 4:7)

Paul was not fighting the Roman Empire, the Sanhedrin, or the Church. Who then was he warring against? Paul fought with the same three enemies that Adam's disobedience sentenced us to contend with - the world, the devil and the flesh. Though his battle was intense with all of these, Romans 7:13-24 lets us know that of the three, Paul's flesh was certainly his nemesis.

Paul wrote more on dying to our carnal nature and its manifestations in the Church, than these other two areas of struggle combined. From his writings in the New Testament, we understand that we can separate ourselves from the world. We can rebuke, resist, and even cast out the devil; but there is only one solution for flesh. It has to die...everyday. The question is how do we accomplish this?

Paul knew the answer.

I have been crucified with Christ; it is no longer I who live, but Christ lives in me; and the life which I now live in the flesh I live by faith in the Son of God, who loved me and gave Himself for me. I do not set aside the grace of God; for if righteousness comes through the law, then Christ died in vain." (Galatians 2:20-21)

For over thirty years, I have heard this passage proclaimed from pulpits. Every time my spirit wanted to shout a resounding *yes*! After a powerful encounter down at the altar, the service ended and I returned to normal life. Interestingly, later in the week, my behavior was so *not* indicative of a man dead to sin. I never understood that the key to unlocking and living as one crucified with Christ is often overlooked. After studying the context of verse 20, I now believe that it is *powerless hype,* unless it is plugged into the spiritual nuclear reactor found in verse 21:

I do not set aside the grace of God...

The Greek word that Paul uses here for "set aside" is *atheteo.* It means to neutralize, violate, cast off, despise...reject. The simple fact is this; it's impossible to overcome sin without grace. It is impossible for Christ to live in and through us without grace. If grace is rejected, sin will abound.

James said when sin is conceived it will bring forth death. Any time flesh is allowed to cast off restraint, it will accelerate unbridled until something dies.

So then, what is the child of God to do with CS Lewis' dragon on our shoulder? We must embrace a new paradigm of an old concept. *Grace was launched from heaven for the abolition of sin, and for the emancipation of all of God's children who dare believe its promise.*

Somewhere along the way, Satan duped us into believing that God's grace was *just* a paintbrush to cover our failures. Nothing is further from the truth. This awesome power of grace was not bestowed to earth to produce *Peter Pan believers* who never mature.

The same grace that came to expunge sin from our hearts, also came to eradicate it from earth…especially out of The Body of Christ! Holiness unto the Lord is not a whimsy of God. On the contrary, it is a direct order from our Commander in Chief.

In our day of being more sensitive to seekers than we are to the Holy Spirit, (*who by the way is most sensitive to seekers,*) not many pulpits will preach this side of grace. (I wonder how many pulpits and pews consistently *live* this side of grace - yours truly included.) My answer to these wherever they exist, is the following caution. When we give an account for our ministry and lives in heaven, we will not be judged by the truth that was comfortable to deliver, but simply by The Truth.

Well then, what is grace? Yes, it is God's power to completely atone for our sin. However, I say there is so much more to it than that! The more encompassing message of grace, as I understand the New Testament is this:

For the believer, grace should be the *vaccine* for sin…not just the *antidote*. (*Please read that again*)

As I began writing this chapter, I felt impressed by the Lord to do a study about antidotes and vaccines, leading me to some amazing discoveries about the relevance of God's grace in our lives. The grace of God is indeed both antidote and vaccine for sin's power; yet for the mature believer, the vaccine model is the victorious message conveyed throughout The New Testament.

You may wonder what I mean. I discovered that antidotes are given to reverse the power of a poison *after* it enters your body. They are often the last hope after venom or poison has begun to destroy tissue. Antidotes are administered after the scorpion stings and the serpent strikes. In the life of a believer, this is indeed *a* work of grace.

In Luke 10 Jesus told his disciples, "Behold, I give you power to tread over serpents and scorpions and over all the power of the enemy, and nothing shall by any means harm you." Many theologians interpret these serpents and scorpions that Jesus mentions, as types of demonic powers.

That said, we may have limited our understanding of this passage to our delineated authority against demonic assaults and schemes against the Body of Christ. Though true, I believe that there is more here than meets the eye, at least as it pertains to grace. God's grace is that remedy, the power we receive to cleanse us from the venom of our sin after being *bitten or stung*, and this absolutely is a manifestation and work of grace for all who believe.

However, vaccines differ from antidotes in that they give the body immunity to a disease *before* exposure. They're not the same as antidotes, because they are preventive strikes against a virus when it attacks the body. The works of Jenner, Pasteur and later Salk in the field of immunization, literally changed the face of medicine and humanity for countless millions. My novice understanding of their work is that for the creation of a vaccine, a host must take on the virus, literally making the virus a part of itself. This host battles and eventually overcomes the power of that virus. This triumph ultimately results in the creation of antibodies that afford immunity to future attacks from the disease.

There is a vaccinating power of grace, (if you will), that I never knew existed. I believe God reveals this vaccine model in 2 Corinthians 5:21, where Paul discusses the atoning work of Calvary. Consider the parallels of the physical and spiritual vaccine models:

God made him, (*Jesus the host*), who had no sin, to become sin for us, (*to be infected with the virus*), so that in him we might become the righteousness of God, (*build immunity to sin*) in Christ Jesus.

Let's say Hallelujah!

If I have lost your attention for a moment, please don't not let my sad attempt at a science lesson distract you from one of the most profound truths in Scripture. Child of God, the Bible clearly supports the fact that God's grace is our antidote after we have been injected with sin's venom.

But much more, the amazing part here is that grace is a *holy inoculation* against the works of our flesh, the lure of the world, and the temptation of evil. It is our Holy Spirit Teflon to the onslaught of wickedness and the world system! To limit God's amazing grace as simply the antidote for our sin is to strip his authority and mandate from these scriptures. Please read and ponder these prayerfully. (Italics mine)

Through him, we have received *grace* and apostleship for

obedience to the faith among all nations for his name, 6

among whom you also are the called of Jesus Christ

(Romans 1:5-7)

So now, brethren, I commend you to God and to the word
of his *grace*, which is *able to build you up* and give you an
inheritance among all those who are *sanctified*.

(Acts 20:32-33)

Do not offer the parts of your body to sin, as instruments of
wickedness, but rather offer yourselves to God, as those who
have been brought from death to life; and offer the parts of
your body to him as instruments of righteousness. 14 *For sin
shall not be your master*, because you are not
under law, *but under grace*.

(Romans 6:13-14 NIV)

These passages imply that grace exists for much more than
simply forgiveness. How many times have we disobeyed and
said to ourselves, "Oh thank God for his grace, I really blew
it."

Yes thank God, but notice this passage in Paul's message to
the Church at Rome, where he reminds us that grace was also
given to empower us to *obey—for obedience, not just when
we disobey the faith*. Hear Galatians 2:21 again…"I do not set
aside the grace of God, for if righteousness could be gained
through the law, Christ died for nothing!"

All of us, including me, are tempted to act as if Christ died for naught. We struggle with resting in the completed work of God's power. Sometimes these Scriptures can be uncomfortable, especially for believers who'd rather stay in the milk stage of the Word—where we're still in the process of learning the basics, the ABC's of our faith. We're still little children, not ready or yet able to discern the meatier revelation of the Word. However, we must mature to the place that requires an understanding that grace's power is far more than a gift at salvation and a recitation before mealtimes. These verses and others demand that we yield to a deeper understanding of the "word of his grace."

God's grace is active and dynamic. It was never meant to enable our sin nature to thrive but to die, and that death is through daily crucifixion. His grace yields the power to die and then live again, as it flows from the very bloodstream of Jesus who is the Resurrection and the Life! This transformation power of grace is a key to our victory over sin.

Simply put, grace is the ability to live out what the Word of God demands; furthermore, the application of God's grace in our lives must equate to change.

Lisa and I have an amazing son named Elliott. His hands are bigger than mine; his shoes are now larger. His intellect surpassed mine a long time ago. He is handsome, an artist, a musician, a brilliant poet and the best son I could ask for. However, for all the growing up he has done, there might be some areas in his behavior that he could possibly—maybe just a little bit if it's not too much to ask—change and do a *tad* better. If you've ever parented a teenager, you know just what I mean.

One rule we strive for in our home is to honor us with first–time obedience when we tell our kids to do something. After now eighteen years, the first time is still often the second or third, (with a privilege being taken away I might add.) My heart's desire for Elliott is not just obedience or conforming to my wishes.

It is the same with God. His desire is not for us to obey, though for most of my life I thought that's all he wanted of me. My greatest hope for Elliott is to continue to *be changed* into the image of his heavenly Father. God's deepest desire for his children is that we are changed into the image of Jesus, our elder brother. The following scripture could easily be embraced as the believer's official job description.

For God knew his people in advance, and he chose them *to become like his Son,* so that his Son would be the firstborn, with many brothers and sisters. (Romans 8:29 NLT)

That's it, the bottom line. It's the core agenda of everything you will need to know about the theology of your Christian walk. We are to continue on in the faith and become progressively more and more like Jesus. In Galatians 3:26-28, Paul gives us a new paradigm of just what happens when we are born again in Christ.

For you are all sons of God through faith in Christ Jesus. For as many of you as were baptized into Christ have put on Christ. There is neither Jew nor Greek, there is neither slave nor free, there is neither male nor female; for you are all one in Christ Jesus.

Paul says that in the Kingdom of God—in a very real sense—we lose our own identity as we embrace Jesus'. Concerning our transformation in his image, I have often wondered why we will be gender and race neutral in Heaven. I now believe it's because one day, when Father God opens up the family photo album, he wants us to be indistinguishable from his firstborn

Son. He wants all his children looking exactly alike. A thought worth pondering, don't you think?

The fact is, that sin produces slavery. Slaves by definition *have to obey*; however, sons change into the image of their father. God's grace is the power for that change. You see, if we view God's holy gift in a common way, then its power in us will eventually become common and negated.

This is not unlike what happened when Jesus went to visit his home town of Nazareth and began preaching in the synagogue. As a young child, Jesus was known around Nazareth, so when he came home to preach, you would have thought that he would have been well-received by family, friends, and neighbors. The exact opposite occurred.

I guess they found it hard to embrace a message from the little boy who used to skip stones into the Sea of Galilee. "Where did this Man get this wisdom and these mighty works? Is this not the carpenter's son? " (Matthew 13:55) In essence they were saying, *"Hey, isn't this Joseph's boy? Yeah, he the one who went to school with us and always seemed to be a little different. Oh I remember, he is the one...the brainiac who always had his head buried in the Torah. I think he and his dad built our coffee table and worked on our room addition...*

wonder worker huh? He could barely carry on a conversation when I knew him."

Obviously, I am taking liberty here, but the fact remains that *Jesus was ordinary to them.* They did not honor the power of his presence; subsequently, they never saw the presence of his power. We often regard grace with that same familiarity.

For years my faith walk existed as a cyclical pattern of sin, confession, forgiveness then repeating the pattern. Year after year I walked in this madness, filled with shame and growing deeper in bondage. I would hear about someone "getting victory," and wonder why that never seemed to happen for me. I became a spiritual chameleon. I could turn on the mighty man of God routine when needed, but inside I lived in spiritual schizophrenia.

Like the '60's television show "To Tell The Truth," the questioned thundered in me, *would the real born again believer please stand up?* Regrettably, I was too often paralyzed by the venom of sin that I mentioned, forever needing that antidote. The dissonance that I felt almost drove me insane. I had to change or abandon all that I had known of God.

I realize now that this cycle occurred because my understanding of his grace was impaired; in fact, it was way off base. As I write this, the thought comes to mind that I never remember being discipled, much less fathered, by anyone that understood and conveyed the two-fold purpose of grace—salvation and sanctification.

Grace for me was always about post-sin trauma. You might be wondering if I think I've *arrived* to the place where my sin doesn't stink. Please, I assure you I am not that naïve. I pray I am not that pharisaical. I am just saying there is a key that can unlock our chains no matter how old the shackles. Personally, I do not want an impotent Savior and would refuse to serve a powerless God. He is neither.

If you receive one truth here, let it be that God has never made an investment in someone and left that person worse than he found them. Like me, you may need a new pair of lenses to view your sin and your God. Try this on for size: all of your sin, bondage, weaknesses and issues have but one size... *smaller than grace*.

You may have lived in abnormal so long that normal seems impossible. If you believe that you are eternally bound in the cycle of sin, I encourage you to discover one of the most liberating truths in scripture, though it might not seem that way at first.

Do you not know that the unrighteous will not inherit the kingdom of God? Do not be deceived. Neither fornicators, nor idolaters, nor adulterers, nor homosexuals, nor sodomites, nor thieves, nor covetous, nor drunkards, nor revilers, nor extortioners will inherit the kingdom of God. And such were some of you.

But you were *washed*, but you were *sanctified*, but you were *justified* in the name of the Lord Jesus and by the Spirit of our God. (1 Corinthians 6:9-11)

Paul's words declare to the Corinthians, You WERE who you WERE but you ARE who you ARE! Washed! Sanctified! Justified!

This passage gives us *the expectation* of grace. Grace has an expectation and that expectation is *transformation*. Paul lists the characteristics of some unbelievers who struggled with evil desires. It's heavy stuff, but he goes on to declare the outcome when grace's power is applied. The Corinthian church had its share of former heathens, and their sins were *biggies!* Then, Paul resounds that they had an encounter. They encountered grace and the power of The Holy Spirit, and wow what a change.

From Genesis to Revelation, the Bible is crammed with grace stories of people who were delivered and transformed.

You and I were/are a _____. Whatever the behavior or sin, it is no match for the spiritual quantum of amazing grace found in the work of the Cross. I must believe this or quit the faith.

There is a grand result of grace and its corresponding works of righteousness and holiness. The writer of Hebrews gives us this charge:

> Pursue peace with all people, and holiness, without which no one will see the Lord.
>
> (Hebrews 12:14)

Notice the verse does not say pursue *righteousness*. If you have accepted Christ as your Lord and Savior, then you are righteous. We're told in 2 Corinthians 5:21 that we are righteous through Jesus substitutionary work on the cross. However, *holiness is something that we are mandated here to pursue*. Righteousness became the condition of our spirit-man in the eyes of Father God when we accepted the finished work of Calvary.

Remember that Ephesians chapter 1, verses 3-6, tells us that Jesus' sacrifice made us Holy, blameless and accepted before the world began; furthermore, God now chooses to view us through this holy covering of the righteous blood of Calvary's Lamb!

My mentor, Steve Franklin, taught me three-fold work of grace in the life of the believer: Grace first empowers our *spirits* to be *reborn*. Next, grace mixed with God's word enables our *souls to be renewed*.

Finally, grace coupled with the fruit of the Spirit, empowers *our bodies to be retrained*. I believe that these latter two are what the author of Hebrews is addressing when he says pursue holiness.

What then is holiness? Holiness is when our internal righteousness on display as we obey God and his word. It is how we live out what God has deposited in our spirits. Because we have been made righteous by grace, then we have no excuse for not pursuing what God deems as holy. I see holiness further defined, as seeking the things that are dear to God and what is congruent with his word. I think holiness can be summed up completely by a recent popular saying that's inscripted on bracelets and screen-printed on T-shirts… "What would Jesus do?"

Psalm 89 tells us that the very pillars of God's throne are judgment and justice. Here is a psalm describing King David's glorious reign and dynasty which God ordained. Righteousness and justice are the foundation of the way God rules in our lives. He is always fair and has never made a bad decision, ever. It is the cruelest of all demands then for the supreme and perfect creator, to require holiness from inferior creation, if that mandate was unattainable.

We see a glimpse of this mandate in the story of the woman caught in adultery in John 8. The Jewish leaders, by arresting the woman without the man involved, already violated the law as both parties were mandated to be stoned.

These leaders wanted to trap Jesus, but instead of falling for it and responding, he wrote on the ground with his finger, and said to them, "let he who is without sin cast the first stone." One by one the accusers left the scene, and Jesus stood alone with the woman in question. "Woman, where are they? Has no one condemned you?" he asks her. "No one, sir," she answers. "Then neither do I condemn you. Go now and sin no more."

We see first hand in this story the dual work of grace. First, Jesus forgives her with grace, saying no one condemns her. He then commands her with the *word of his grace* to stop sinning. After their encounter, Jesus gives his disciples an often-overlooked truth. "He who follows me shall not walk in darkness." Jesus' words and the Apostle Paul's are unmistakably similar.

For sin shall not be your master, because you are not under

law, but under grace. (Romans 6:14)

This woman had a power encounter with the grace giver. He forgave her with grace. He then commanded her as he does us through his word. Go and grow in grace and cease from continual sinning.

Grace is a favorite topic among believers, yet so many Christians misunderstand it, or at least haven't fully embraced its power. God's grace is a gift. It is yours and mine to appropriate at any temptation moment. Grace comes to us freely; however, James tells us that its power multiplies in our lives through humility.

But he gives us more and more grace (power of the Holy

Spirit, to meet this evil tendency and all others fully). That is

why he says, God sets himself against the proud and haughty,

but gives grace [continually] to the lowly (those who are

humble enough to receive it). James 4:6 AMP

An attitude of humility is essential. Satan knows from personal experience that pride separates us from the presence of God. I once heard Derek Prince, a brilliant bible teacher who passed away in 2003, say that *"pride may be the only sin that Satan will not condemn you for!"*

Wow! What a bombshell. If we blow it through anger, lust, greed, etc, the devil will beat us senseless though condemnation. Not true with pride. I can honestly say that Satan has never even once berated me about the pride thing. He does just the opposite.

He convinces us that we are more humble than most believers we know. Everyone else sure needs to change, but you and I are just dandy. There's a bit of self-righteousness in all of us who strive to keep the rules. It's so easy to slip into a critical spirit as Satan blinds us to the giant sequoia in our own eye as we attempt to remove the splinter from our neighbor's. What makes God despise pride so much?

Pride is so dangerous because it is the coronary disease of our spiritual hearts. It is the *eternal* silent killer.

Proverbs warns us that pride is the prelude to destruction and that a haughty spirit precedes a fall. Lisa gave me an amazing insight about falling away from God because of pride. "Jon, it's hard for someone to fall if they are consistently prostrate on their face before God." I thank my wife for reminding me of this truth. Not only does pride foreshadow destruction, the apostle Peter says it literally positions God against us.

God sets Himself against the proud (the insolent, the over-bearing, the disdainful, the presumptuous, the boastful)—[and he opposes, frustrates, and defeats them], but gives grace (favor, blessing) to the humble. (1 Peter 5:5 AMP)

He should know. Before he was the Apostle Paul, he was Saul of Tarsus and hated Christians. He made it his goal to capture and bring Christians to public trial and execution.

Saul was present when Stephen, the first Christian martyr was killed by an angry mob. Here was a man who excelled at his career. Do you think he was a man filled with pride? Absolutely, and his Damascus road experience that left him blind for three days humbled him and changed his life and the course of history.

I don't know about you, but facing God in the ring is not how I want to start my day. It does not have to be this way. The great truth is that he is wants to continue to be *for* us. The problem is that our sin separates us from fellowship with him, and we lose the ability to perceive just *how much he is for us!*

The word says that if he is on our side, who could ever stand against us? He is indeed for us, even in our failures. Back in Chapter two, we talked about God's *unconditional, undiminished* and *unrelenting love*. However, we can do so much more if we are with him, walking in fellowship and keeping ourselves from sin and the entrapments of this world. If you have lived below the expectation of grace, I challenge you to repent.

If you were sitting across the table sharing a cup of coffee with me right now, I would pray over you with these words, "Awake from the anesthesia of apathy to sin." I challenge you to honor your pedigree and family crest, the Shield of Faith. Change the way you think about this amazing gift of God and this under-appreciated weapon against darkness. You have been born from above to conquer here below!

If this is not your experience, in the mighty name of Jesus I call you out of bondage. I call you out of the cycle of brokenness and shame. If he can continually do it for me, he can and will do it for you! Eugene O'Neill, American playwright said this: *Man is born broken. He lives by mending. The grace of God is the glue.* May his grace come alive in you!

As I end this chapter, I want to leave you with some of my favorite passages about grace and its power.

These truths have strengthened my walk and resolve to leave *Peter Pan and Neverland* behind, and grow up in the grace and knowledge of The Lord Jesus Christ:

For whatever is born of God overcomes the world. And this is the victory that has overcome the world — our faith. Who is he who overcomes the world, but he who believes that Jesus is the Son of God? (1 John 5:4-5)

We know that whoever is born of God does not sin; but he who has been born of God keeps himself, and the wicked one does not touch him.
(1 John 5:18)

You, dear children, are from God and have overcome them, because the one who is in you is greater than the one who is in the world.
(1 John 4:4 NIV)

Therefore, gird up the loins of your mind, be sober, and rest your hope fully upon the grace that is to be brought to you at the revelation of Jesus Christ; as obedient children, not conforming yourselves to the former lusts, as in your ignorance; but as he who called you is holy, you also be holy

in all your conduct, 16 because it is written,

"be holy, for I am holy."

(1 Peter 1:13-16)

For the grace of God that brings salvation has appeared to all

men, teaching us that, denying ungodliness and worldly lusts,

we should live soberly, righteously, and Godly

in the present age

(Titus 2:11-12)

Chapter 9

Cover Me, I'm Goin' in!

You were the anointed cherub who *covers*; I established you; You were on the holy mountain of God; You walked back and forth in the midst of fiery stones....Therefore I cast you as a profane thing out of the mountain of God; And I destroyed you, O *covering* cherub, From the midst

of the fiery stones

(Ezekiel 28:14, 160

Obey those who rule over you, and be submissive, for they watch out for your souls, as those who must give account. Let them do so with joy and not with grief, for that would be unprofitable for you.

(Hebrews 13:17)

Through Him, we have received grace and apostleship for obedience to the faith among all nations for his name, among whom you also are the called of Jesus Christ

(Romans 1:5-7)

Then the LORD God called to Adam and said to him,

"Where are you?"

(Genesis 3:9)

I n nearly every war movie or law enforcement drama, you'll hear this phrase - "Cover me, I'm goin' in!" "Cover me" is blurted out as one of the *good* guys advances his position against the *bad* guys. Hollywood has used a moment of crisis to add sensation and suspense, but the principle of being covered or watched over for God's children is critical nonetheless.

I define covering as submission to oversight, counsel, or wisdom from others, and I assure you it is essential for the child of God who wants to walk in freedom and victory.

Al Yother, a good friend and former CFO of one of the ten largest banks in America, once said to me, "Jon, It's not what is *expected*, but what is *inspected* that develops character in us."

Isaiah 58:8 talks about the glory of the Lord being our rear guard and Psalm 91 declares that we can abide under the shadow of his wings. Both of these allusions paint a picture of our Father overshadowing and protecting us. He indeed does have us covered and will guard our "backs" as we move forward in life. However, throughout his word, God often used human voices of wisdom as well, to steer his people in paths of righteousness when the horizon was bleak and the future unsure.

John Donne, in his Meditation XVII says it best, "No man is an island entire to himself." Donne understood a principle that God actually instituted at creation. Our God designed his first family with accountability in mind. We now know the terrible price humanity paid when Eve and then Adam, failed to honor their Father's counsel. The truth Donne spoke is wise for us to heed because Isolation is lethal.

Fellowship is one of God's purposes for us. We are meant for companionship and have a need to belong. Our father knows we need others to help us make wise decisions when we are at those crossroads in our lives. He places in our lives mentors, accountability partners, and wise friends who can speak the truth in love. These, in addition to his Holy Spirit, provide covering over us.

With that said, let me begin this chapter by asking you three questions.

1. Who have you *intentionally* placed in your life that can tell you *no, this isn't a wise choice*?
2. Do you have counsel that will love you enough to correct you when you are wrong?
3. The third and *most important* question is this… If your trusted counsel told you no, or that you were in error, would you listen and then change your direction?

For various reasons, these Biblical figures did not have, or chose not honor, a voice in their lives to challenge their wrong decisions.

Consider their consequences:

Abraham - Ishmael…Hamas, Hussein, Bin Laden, 9/11

Ten spies - Three million graves in the wilderness

Samson - A really, *really bad hair day*

Saul - Kingdom stripped, family destroyed

David - Bathsheba, Uriah, Tamar, Absalom

Solomon - One unfulfilled king, 1000 unhappy wives.

Judas - Robbery, betrayal, suicide

On and on we could cite stories, Biblical and otherwise, of people who chose not to invite a voice of reason or covering in their lives; subsequently, they made wrong choices that have polluted the landscape of history.

This chapter may be the most difficult one for me to write. It includes pain that could and should have been avoided. I own the truth that every major failure I have made as an adult has been primarily for two reasons: either a prayer failure, or a failure to seek counsel from those who have "been there," who gained wisdom through their pain and have the scars to prove it. I now know that we acquire wisdom one of two ways: through a mentor or through a mess. Although this first path is the least painful and is our Father's obvious choice, our fallen nature invariably resists correction.

On ten occasions in scripture God tells his people that he sets before them life and death, blessing and cursing, as to whether they will obey him or not.

He presents them with the option to remain under his covering. His word chronicles both the wonderful and devastating results of their free will. Since creation, God has always afforded freethinking to his children. I have heard it said that love without options is not love at all. I agree, but more than that, I believe that the single most important gift humanity ever received from God was *choice*.

Choice elevated us above every other creature at Genesis; ultimately, it affords us eternal life or allows us to descend into damnation. Choice by definition brings consequences. Consequences necessitate accountability. The true response to biblical accountability always requires submission, and genuine submission begins with humility. I have found that it is the humility part that we often find hard to swallow.

Throughout his word, God has required his people to seek counsel before action, even if his chosen vessel at the time seemed larger than life. Consider Moses. He is the first person we know of in scripture to hear the audible voice of God since the days of Abraham, Isaac, and Jacob. In Exodus chapter three, God appears to him in the miracle of the burning bush. God tells Moses that from that point on, *he* will be the designated representative for the creator in the universe. God also gives Moses the emancipation orders to deliver Israel from Egyptian bondage. In their dialogue, God reveals Himself and his relationship with the patriarchs of Moses' faith. This assures Moses that *this* God can underwrite the stuttering shepherd's new assignment. This also places Moses in a unique category. He joins the elite trio of Abraham, Isaac, and Jacob, as one who has personally met Yahweh, The I AM! After their encounter, God gives Moses some instructions that are relevant to our discussion in this chapter.

Go and gather the elders of Israel together, and say to them, 'The LORD God of your fathers, the God of Abraham, of Isaac, and of Jacob, appeared to me, saying, "I have surely visited you and seen what is done to you in Egypt. (Exodus 3:16-17)

God tells Moses to go and show himself to the elders of Israel and clue them in on the Exodus plan. Now, there were obviously many reasons for this instruction, but what I see worth noting, is that God did not allow Moses, though *anointed and appointed*, to circumvent the eldership covering that existed in Israel.

Although these elders had not seen or heard from "I AM" in four-hundred plus years, and though Moses was God's man of the hour, our Father knew that Moses would need *their* blessing and covering to complete his assignment. No matter what magnitude of revelation Moses had of God, his experience had to be subject to examination. The same must be true today.

Revelation must always be subject to evaluation.

May I step back up on my soapbox for a second? Concerning revelation, it is interesting to me to observe ministers who appear to be caught up by their *elite anointing* and level of revelation. I say this because; revelation by definition is proof of either one or both of these conditions: *ignorance or inaccuracy.*

Every time God has revealed anything to anyone, it is because they were unaware of the concept or he was correcting erroneous thoughts held about him and his word. Therefore, revelation should be delivered from the posture and pulpit of humility, thanking God that he has enlightened our dullness or corrected our misunderstanding!

Solomon, the wisest man who ever lived, urges us over and again to "get wisdom." God's wisdom *is* revelation of God's ways. Solomon's admonition is rooted in the wisdom of his own father's words from Psalm 100, "It is he that hath made us and not vice versa."

If we examine just the last fifty years, we have witnessed a sad parade of ministers and believers who believed their knowledge, anointing, or revelation, exempted them from evaluation.

In each case without fail, covering or apostleship has been absent or inept. As we learned in Chapter 5, this happens because Adam's children love our gifts being heralded but too often refrain from *fruit* inspection.

The results have been disastrous to the cause of Christ. It is amazing to me that in the world of finance and business; we have infrastructures in place to ensure integrity. However, often no such infrastructure exists in the Body of Christ for morality, where our goal is not "black" profit and loss statements, but influencing eternal destinies.

When Lisa and I purchased our first home in 1996, we were thrilled to finally have a piece of the American Dream. Our mortgage payment for this 1,700 square foot *castle* was $932.00 a month. The payment was a bit of a stretch, but we knew we could pinch our pennies and make it work.

We had *moved on up* just like the Jeffersons, the 70's sitcom about George and Louise Jefferson, an upper-middle class African American couple. The show's theme song talked about movin' on up to the east side, to a deluxe apartment in the sky, and at the end they say, "We finally got a piece of the pie."

Our piece of the pie began to crumble two years later. My poor financial management of credit cards and frivolous expenditures necessitated that we get a second mortgage. Soon enough this wasn't enough money to make it work, so refinance number three came two years later. The slight stretch of the first payment had now become the *thinning of my sanity* to the tune of $1,500.00 more a month!

Every day decent people working their post at collection agencies hounded us by telephone. We dreaded checking the mail. We often realized a bill was due only after the service or utility was terminated. We were in hell and ignorant of how to escape. If you've been there, you understand. If you haven't been there, count your blessings.

The sad truth is that I had a father who was financially sound, a brother who was on his way to being a millionaire, and a father-in-law who chaired the Mississippi Savings and Loan board for eleven years. "Einstein" here, who once thought he was pretty good at managing a family, had failed to seek out counsel on any of these fiscal decisions from the financial brains in my own life. What went wrong? Among many other things, my pride and machismo told me to do it my way. After all, my family doesn't need to know my business.

The deeper and more painful truth is that I did not want any of these men whom I looked up to, to know how badly I had failed. I just wanted to be successful in their eyes. Sadly, *my way* to success did not work as well as it did for Sinatra. The stench of my ignorance still wafts from my credit report today. The whole mess was avoidable had I simply sought—and heeded—wise counsel.

About eight years ago, a precocious and precious little red-headed boy lived across the street from us. Ben prided his autonomy as most five year olds do; so much so, that you could not address him merely as "Ben," but you had to call him... *"Big to do it Ben!"* We would jokingly ask him if he would help us with this chore or with that task. As his cherubic face lit up he would reply with a lisp, "Yes sir, *I'm Big to do it Ben!*"

Ben's *wisdom* though adorable, began in a place called Eden, where Adam and Eve assumed that they too were "big enough to do it" outside of the instructions of their creator. Humanity has endured incalculable suffering ever since. Israel's first king had this problem as well. When Saul finally lost the reins of the throne, the prophet Samuel said to him, "When you were *small* in your own eyes, God made you king over Israel."

Neither Saul, little Ben, or any of us are big enough to do *life* in our own strength, wisdom, or knowledge. It is here where covering exists to protect us. This covering is essential for our spiritual development as we mature as sons and daughters of God.

Through Him, we have received grace and apostleship for obedience to the faith among all nations for his name, among whom you also are the called of Jesus Christ (Romans 1:5-7)

We've already examined the first part of this Romans' passage that pertained to the power of grace to conquer sin in our lives, however to live in divine order, we cannot omit Paul's second requisite for Godly living. He says that we have also received *apostleship* to remain obedient to the faith. What then is apostleship? I define it this way:

Apostleship, is the collection of Godly voices in our lives to which we submit our sin-struggles and wisdom-deficit issues.

Notice I said "collection" of godly voices. Proverbs 11:14 teaches us that wisdom and safety are found when we in seek multiple voices of counsel. This construct is readily seen in Jewish culture with something called the minyan. The minyan, whose origin stems all the way back to the Torah, is a group of 10 men. In addition to the requirement of their presence to initiate religious services and meetings, they also serve as voices of counsel for the younger men as they grow from age 13 at Bar mitzvah, to grown men or full stature in the Jewish tradition.

This minyan provides counsel for the young Jewish man as he navigates through the challenges and choices of life. They help him weigh the best case, worst case scenarios of his choices, but leave the ultimate decision to him. Wow, do you think we gentiles could learn from this brilliant practice of multiple voices of counsel?

Looking back again to Paul's words to the church at Rome, He says we need grace and apostleship to remain obedient to the faith. I see *grace* then as *internal power* and *apostleship* as *external accountability or covering*.

The two of these working in tandem is God's double insulation from the deception of sin and the shipwrecking of our faith. Why is apostleship imperative for the children of God?

Apostleship requires that we answer for integrity here as it prepares us for our inevitable Q & A at the Judgment Seat of Christ.

This upcoming *appointment* reminds us that accountability is eternal. Very simply, apostleship or covering should not only encourage, exhort and confirm us, but should also assist us in examining the morality of our thoughts and deeds.

Let's examine another "covering" passage that is often ignored in today's churches.

Obey those who rule over you, and be submissive, for they watch out for your souls, as those who must give account. Let them do so with joy and not with grief, for that would be unprofitable for you. (Hebrews 13:17)

This passage from Hebrews sometimes makes me uncomfortable, yet I cannot omit its truth or relevance in my life, I do realize that many zealots have taken this passage and imposed unnecessary and even worse, ungodly demands on the Body of Christ. I will address these abuses later on; however, we must understand that author is not *suggesting* that we heed Godly counsel, he *commands it*. He underscores the need for covering by saying that those in spiritual authority are stewards for our very souls. They have a vested interest in shepherding us, as they will be judged more intensely for their effectiveness or failures in stewarding the lives entrusted to their care.

Ok, if this mandate for covering exists, then why the disparity of what we know to be right and what exists in the Body, with its untold spiritual casualties? The reasons are many, but I will try to illuminate a couple that I perceive.

To begin with, too many churches today have become social hot spots where relationships are so surface, that *any* imperatives to *seekers* would be deemed much too old fashioned and constrictive. Yet in this passage, Godly correction is a given.

Actually, if we really embrace the collective message of Jesus' life, we understand that he was *constrictive* to the extreme; death to self and to all that the world deemed precious. *Jesus was however a sensitive seeker*. He was *sensitive* to obey his father's voice and *sought* only to do his Father's will. I do hope we will re-adapt his model for church.

To our shame, the operation of this Hebrews passage is rarely observed because the Church has lost the treasure of confidentiality. Instead of bearing each other's most secret burdens, we promise to pray over them and then we gossip carelessly and destroy our credibility. We are all guilty of this at times. In the name of prayer requests, we share the most intimate details of someone's life to complete strangers. This irresponsibility has resulted in too many sheep leaving the faith wounded and bitter, who now have contempt for Christ and Christians. The world notices. Mahatma Gandhi once said, "I do not reject your Christ, I love your Christ. It is just that so many of you Christians are so unlike your Christ."[12]

I wonder how many countless others have seen our disingenuous faith and felt the same way? Jesus told us that his progeny would have one irrefutable *birthmark* - Agape towards one another. Agape in the Church was designed to cover a multitude of sins and heal brokenness in the Body. This may not be your experience. If the Church has wounded you, I encourage you not to abandon it completely.

Our adversary made that mistake first, and remember where it got him. As I wrote in Chapter Two, Satan voluntarily severed his connection to our Father, and he is hell-bent, (*sorry, I couldn't resist*), on causing you to do likewise. He is an opportunist and would love nothing more than to capitalize on your wounding.

Give him and inch and he will take far more than a mile. Satan wants *eternity*. He wants you ruined, and I assure you he has studied us well enough to implement a strategy to make this happen. Remember that Lucifer fell first. He knows far more than we do about the purpose and power of covering. The following verses from the book of Ezekiel allow us to peer into a sliver of his job description in heaven. No other place in scripture do we get the opportunity to understand what our adversary did in his former life. Here, God permits our glance into a window of eternity past.

I was astounded when I actually grasped what the Bible describes as a primary function of Lucifer's heavenly assignment.

You were the **anointed cherub who** *covers*; I established you; You were on the holy mountain of God; You walked back and forth in the midst of fiery stones. ...Therefore I cast you as a profane thing out of the mountain of God; And I destroyed you, **O** *covering* **cherub**, From the midst of the fiery stones Ezekiel 28:14,16

The word *established,* as mentioned above in verse 14, is a very interesting Hebrew word. Among other things, it conveys the idea: to give, to trust, entrust an assignment and even to employ. Lucifer was so highly esteemed in the eyes of God, that The Father *trusted* him...but what did God entrust to him. **God trusted Lucifer to maintain covering**. Even more, this 14th verse tells us that Satan literally *flowed in the anointing as he covered.*

Now, I am not enough the scholar to expound on all we can glean from this discourse in Ezekiel. However, when the Holy

Spirit instructs Ezekiel to mention this fact twice, that Satan's job description in heaven was to *cover*, then we need to investigate what covering entails.

We also better understand that he wants us *uncovered*! I have tried not to bury you with an excessive amount of Hebrew or Greek word study.

However, I do believe it is critical that we comprehend what the Hebrew meaning is for both of these covering references. The word Ezekiel used for cover and covering is the Hebrew word "cakak." Some of its definitions are as follows:

- To hedge, fence about, shut in
- To block, to overshadow, to screen
- To stop the approach
- To cover
- To shut off
- To cover oneself
- To be a protector
- To cover as to lay over
- To weave together, to weave

God entrusted an assignment to Satan in heaven that we could not begin to comprehend. I am unable to fully fathom what in heaven would ever need guarding, fencing in, stopping the approach to, or shutting off... *but I think I might have an idea.*

Psychologists tell us that human nature craves and covets that which is closest to us, yet *just out of our reach.* We usually do not desire the things that are way beyond our grasp or socio economic status, but tend more to covet the familiar. For example, we see a neighbor's new car, a friend's new house, or a coworker's position and want them so much that we sometimes cry unfair! God obviously understood psychology long before there were psychologists. He underscored what therapists now know, and communicated it in Exodus Chapter 20.

You shall not covet your neighbor's house. You shall not covet your neighbor's wife, or his manservant or maidservant, his ox or donkey, or anything that belongs to your neighbor."
(Exodus 20:17 NIV)

Our Father knew that with the Israelites and with us, covetousness occurs with those things that we often see, yet that are slightly out of bounds. Lucifer fell when he yearned for something that only God possessed. If what we understand about coveting and human behavior is true, could it also be accurate of angelic conduct? In Heaven's domain, what single bestow-ment is God's alone? The answer is this: In heaven's borders, God alone gets all the *glory*.

This 14th verse of Ezekiel 28, informs us that Lucifer dwelt in a special place upon the holy mountain of God. It appears that he had unique access to the Trinity, not enjoyed by any other of his kind. With his constant exposure to ceaseless ado-ration of the Godhead, I believe it was Lucifer's unique van-tage point that caused him to fall. The Bible declares that all of heaven is incessantly filled with swells of shouts, songs, and celebrations that have one focus…*Glory to God in the highest!*

Now imagine Lucifer as he beheld God, his vista of unattain-able glory never altering. As glorious as he was, as privileged above his peers he may have been, his luster was pathetically pale compared to him who sits enthroned in splendor on the sides of the North. All glory, adulation and conceivable praise to Almighty God were right there, incessantly passing before Lucifer's eyes. We now know that at some point his eyes closed, looked inward, and turned *green*. Again, as in Exodus, the glory he wanted was so close yet so far away. Considering his vantage point and heavenly assignment that we just exam-ined, could it be that Lucifer had the sole duty to *defend, pro-tect, and stop anything from getting too close to,* Jehovah's *glory?* Was it there, as a sentinel of God's glory, that Lucifer attempted to seize the uncontainable, and thus stumbled into eternal banishment?

We do know that Paul tells us in Romans that all have sinned and fallen short of the glory of God. If sin causes us to fall short of the glory, then surely the first sin caused the first sinner to *fall short of the glory as well,* and what a fall it was.

Ok, I will put theology and conjecture away, but it is fun to wonder, isn't it? I do know this; Satan is eternally fixated upon you and me leaving the shelter of God's glory and seeking our own; even better, giving it to him. It also makes sense, that if we leave the umbrella of God's protection, then we are visible and vulnerable to the assaults of darkness. I've experienced this first-hand, and I never want to go back there.

In the introduction to Psalm 91, the psalmist says that *he who dwells in the secret place of the Most High, shall abide under the shadow of the Almighty.*

The word *secret place* here is the Hebrew word "cether." Let's compare some of its meanings back to Lucifer's assignment in heaven.

- A covering
- A cover

- A shelter
- A hiding place
- Secrecy

Lucifer once dwelled in this most holy place of protection. He understands the impenetrable fortress that God is, and that his covering presence provides. His quest is that you and I live *uncovered*, apart from the defense that divine covering affords.

As I mentioned earlier, I am aware that this concept of covering has been a source of much contention and wounding in the Body of Christ. Some ministers and sects of Christianity have taken a good principle to the extreme, subjecting believers to legalism reminiscent of the Pharisees and even worse. You may be one of the casualties of unbiblical, or maybe even abusive spiritual authority. Again, I plead with you not to abandon biblically-based accountability.

I have to believe that Satan *smells* a wounded or uncovered believer as a lion does bleeding prey.

Nature reveals to us, that it is the isolated or injured animal that the lions devour. *There is a spiritual Serengeti as well.* And Satan, our adversary, walks about like a roaring lion, seeking whom he may devour. (1 Peter 5:8) So we are to be diligent and on guard.

If you study Peter's warning, its context is not coincidental. The Holy Spirit inserts this admonition while addressing issues such as pastoral care, covering, submission to authority, and remaining in the faith. He also specifically addresses pride, as this is a huge impediment to us receiving correction as well. Again, pride caused Satan's fall and it is the silent killer to the believer's spirit.

Well Jon, where do we find this type of protection and what should it look like, you might ask? You may not like my answer. As broken as it has sometimes been, (and God knew it would get that way), the Holy Spirit still instructs us to stay connected to one another in an assembled manner, a church of some kind.

Not forsaking or neglecting to assemble together |as believers|, as is the habit of some people, but admonishing (warning, urging, and encouraging) one another, and all the more faithfully as you see the day approaching.
(Hebrews 10:25 AMP)

Our Father knew that we would unwittingly— and sometimes intentionally—be prone to cease fellowship with one another. Maybe we're too busy, we relocate to a new city, and we get our sensitive feelings hurt in a small group study. The reasons are plentiful, but it's at these times we are the most vulnerable.

Not only do we need a group of believers that we entrust our hearts and weaknesses to, we also need the corporate benefit of the Body and her intercession.

This corporate *covering* is not found solely in the confines of a building with brick and mortar. As I alluded to earlier, there are churches where I would not disclose the secrets of my soul.

However, there is wisdom in numbers and a communal protection for the *herd*—if you will—that manifests when a group of believers walk in transparency and love.

Fritz Perls is one of the cofounders of a stream of psychology known as Gestalt Therapy. One theme you will hear repeatedly in the Gestalt camp is this: "The whole is greater than the sum of its parts." *I believe that this stream of thought is the spirit of the function of the New Testament church.* Over and again, God's word informs us that the collective wisdom of The Body shields us from literal and spiritual blind spots. Remember Solomon's words. *Where there is no counsel, the people fall; but in the multitude of counselors there is safety.* (Proverbs 11:14)

The Hebrew word used here for fall, is *nawfal*. This word means to fail, to flounder, to stumble, to be cast down, and to lose position. *Lose position*, how many ministers and others, have lost their positions in the Kingdom when covering was neglected or rejected? Considering then the Gestalt model of scripture, one main consideration of The Church must be that the collective wisdom of the *whole* of the Body is superlative to the individual mind and choices of us, its members - *the sum of its parts*.

Not only is their wisdom, but there are God-lessons we will never learn apart from one another; even more, there are multiple commandments in the Bible which we cannot obey living outside of fellowship with other believers. I challenge you to try obeying these on your own.

- Serve one another   (Galatians 5:13)
- Accept one another   (Romans 15:7)
- Forgive one another   (Colossians 3:13)
- Greet one another   (Romans 16:16)
- Bear one another's burdens   (Galatians 6:2)
- Be devoted to one another   (Romans 12:10)
- Honor one another   (Romans 12:10)
- Teach one another   (Romans 15:14)

- Submit to one another   (Ephesians 5:21)
- Encourage one another   (1 Thessalonians 5:11)

These mandates are impossible to fulfill if we sequester ourselves from one another, making only brief appearances with cursory conversations on Sunday morning. Body life cannot happen in the circle of *just* you. Rick Warren, author of the best-selling *Purpose Driven Life*, has taught us that a Kingdom mandate for all believers is to peer outside of ourselves and invest in *some-things* and *some-ones* larger than us.

There is an even greater reason for gathering together than these above stated commandments. When we come together to experience biblically ordered and Spirit-led worship, we position ourselves to not only receive his blessings, but also to actually access God's glory.

For the last 6 years, Lisa and I have met every Tuesday for 3 hours with a precious group of women whose ages span from twenty to the mid eighties. We have had the most amazing times in the presence of The Lord. This group of spiritually seasoned women have sat under our ministry, supported us, cried with us, laughed with us, interceded with us; but most importantly, have covered and corrected us as we have grown as ministers. Some of them have been walking with The Lord for 60 years, and they will quickly set us straight if we get off track…and I praise God for them!

We all need these kinds of saints in our lives, not just for covering, but to experience God in a deeper way than we could ever on our own. What do I mean?

Throughout history, we understand that God has blessed *individuals* who obey him. However, it was more often in a corporate setting of obedience, where God chose to manifest his glory.

It is in this glory where we truly experience the transformation he desires. This should be our ultimate prize. When the Apostle Paul addressed the church at Corinth he talked about this manifestation of glory of the Lord:

But we all, with unveiled face, beholding as in a mirror the glory of the Lord, are being transformed into the same image from glory to glory, just as by the Spirit of the Lord.

(2 Corinthians 3:17-18)

Paul is saying that God's glory brings a fresh revelation of himself. In this revelation, we behold new facets of his nature, which magnify what we are *not*. Some may wonder, can't this change occur as effectively when I am alone with

God? It sounds reasonable that we can experience a measure of renewal into Christ image through personal discipleship and worship, but we still need each other for our blind spots. Notice that Paul uses the words *we* and *all* in this verse.

The goal of experiencing God's glory corporately is *group transformation*. It's in this assembled dynamic where we can see far more of Christ as reflected by the many, than we could ever experience through worshiping alone. Iron sharpens iron and a one faceted diamond will never be brilliant. The church is still the answer.

I once heard Dr. Paul Walker, Pastor Emeritus of Mount Paran Church of God in Atlanta, say, "We have one gospel that was given 2000 years ago, but in America, we now have over 500,000 unique delivery systems." God has so blessed our nation, that we all have exponentially more choices than any other people group at any other time to worship him. We have no excuse for not connecting with believers of like faith and like spiritual *DNA*.

Our pastor's wife said something recently that connected with my spirit. She said that each church, and maybe even denomination, has a unique *grace* upon it.

Some churches have a grace of evangelism, some experiential worship, and some a great grace for teaching, etc. I believe that one interpretation from the above mentioned charge from Hebrews, is that we find the *grace place* that connects with what God is doing in our lives. We plant ourselves there, and grow into the maturity of Christ that Paul speaks about in the fourth chapter of Ephesians.

It grieves me that so many have resisted or left covering because of disingenuous and even immoral shepherds. Sheep have suffered. However, there are scores of biblically sound models in countless churches and fellowships across America, some of which are likely in your own neighborhood. I'm not trying to persuade you to seek out a particular form of covering. In fact, John Bevere wrote an excellent book titled *Under Cover*, which illuminates far more that I ever could on the subject. However I do have some practical thoughts on what I believe covering should look like in our lives.

First, I find no place in the Bible where godly covering is dictatorial. For it to accomplish its goal, it must flow through love. Jesus' leadership style is always the standard, and the full counsel of God's Word should serve as our guide. I firmly believe that effective covering must flow out of covenant relationships.

Earlier in the book I addressed covenant in the context of our relationship with God through Christ. Now I want to talk about it in the context of our relationships with one another. Steve Franklin, my friend and mentor whom I have mentioned throughout this work, taught me that every relationship we operate in could be categorized into one of these three types: casual, committed, or covenant. These levels all have parameters and increased degrees of responsibility.

Casual relationships, are those in which we have a common *interest*. Examples of this type are people with whom you interact infrequently. Maybe your kids play for the same ball team, or you work in the same office. These relationships are cursory and you have little or no meaningful interpersonal exchanges.

The next level of relationships goes a bit deeper. These relationships are hallmarked by *commitment*. **In committed relationships, there is not only mutual *interest*, but also an understanding of mutual *investment* into one another.** This most often is observed in the paradigm or employer and employee. You as the employee are committed to your job and the company's mission. You invest your time and skills and in turn, your employer invests monetarily back into you through paychecks, benefits, etc. You obviously have a common interest, but you are connected more through a reciprocal investment.

The third and most significant relationships we have are much more exclusive. **These relationships are covenant commitments.** There is no greater or deeper relationship than covenant. In these relationships there is mutual interest and investment.

But only covenant has access to experience our intimacy. Covenant is precious and is not available to everyone. As believers, we are obviously first in covenant with God through Christ our Lord. If you are married, your spouse always comes second. If you are a parent, your children come next, and then the Church, your career, friends, on down the line. In addition, I believe each of these should receive your time in this diminished order of importance.

Before moving on, I'd like to segue to offer a quick diagnosis and treatment protocol for every marriage that is currently, or has been in distress. I offer this advice because as in finances, I learned this lesson the hard way over the last twenty years. Lisa and I have had our struggles, and by toughing it out and humbling ourselves we've gained insights on making stressful marriages work.

In every troubled marriage, at least one partner if not both, has placed *covenant emphasis* on either a casual or a committed relationship. The remedy is simple, but it requires we give over our will.

It means realigning and recommitting our intimate allegiance to the order that is set forth in God's word. As we do this, we have the assurance of "all things being added unto our lives."

I have had to learn the hard way that my relationship with Lisa is paramount to any other person in this earth, including those who support our ministry the most. Lisa once said to me, "Jon, I wish I was a monthly supporting partner of Jon Potter Ministries, you'd have enough time for me then wouldn't you." Ouch, what a stinging but very needed reprimand of where I had become much too busy, placing covenant emphasis on priorities that never should have eclipsed the relationship with my wife and best friend!

There are some practical issues concerning covering as well. I strongly urge you to connect with covering in the context of covenant relationships. Lisa and I chose this model as we sought to select our board of overseers for our ministry. We asked people who have seen us at our best and worst to be the ones who would shepherd us as our ministry evolved. We wanted those that were "for" us and our decisions, yet would correct us if we veered off track in spiritual and fiscal decisions.

This level of mutual covenant commitment with our elders has spared us from much pain and embarrassment.

Let's unveil a few principles of what that relationship might look like for you. Because we have purposely placed ourselves in submission to covenant relationships, they not only *confirm* us and *cover* us, but also have the right to *confront* us when needed. It is in this area of confrontation, where I believe many covering mishaps have occurred.

The first and best example is found in the story of the *granddaddy* of all sins. Not long after Adam altered the course of humanity, we see how God modeled confrontation within the first covenant relationship.

Of all the things God could have said or done to discipline his children, he first simply asks the following question: "Then the LORD God called to Adam and said to him, "Where are you?" (Genesis 3:9)

What a question, *where are you?* This questions cuts to the quick. Where is your heart? What are your motives? What are your dreams? How are you and is everything okay in your life? In reality, we know that God was not concerned about Adam and Eve's latitude and longitude coordinates. He knew exactly where they were positioned at that moment. The very fact that

God asked this question of his son was indicative that Adam had lost his *relational* direction.

And if we are not careful, we can do the same; overlook the most wonderful dynamic of covering, which actually occurs right after God confronts his son. There in Genesis, God models the archetype for confrontation in all types of relationships. He seeks out Adam. He confronts Adam. He then covers his children. From that point of Adam and humanity's greatest defeat, God then initiates his most amazing and industrious project, redemption of Adam's race…redemption of mankind!

God's heart was and always will be the perpetuation of relationship, regardless of the magnitude of the failure and disappointment we bring.

If you want to submit to a covering, and I hope you do, there's a time to talk about expectations on both ends. And should you fail down the line, remember that restoration is at the heart of Father God. He knew that with Adam—as with us—failure is inevitable. In my experience with three prominent denominations, I have yet to be "wowed" by any of their restoration initiatives that fulfill Paul's commandment to the church at Galatia:

Brethren, if a man is overtaken in any trespass, you who

are spiritual restore such a one in a spirit of gentleness,

considering yourself lest you also

be tempted. (Galatians 6:1)

It has been more my experience than not, that the one who has been *overtaken* with a trespass, is usually *over trodden*, and then forgotten by the establishment that he or she poured their lives into. Even so, there are life-giving groups that can provide you with a healthy balance of camaraderie, counsel and—when necessary—correction. Maybe there is a Christian brother or sister who needs encouragement from you right now.

A great example of God's way of covering is found in the story of Joseph and his confrontation with his brothers found in Genesis chapter 45. Joseph, the dreamer, who was sold into slavery by his jealous brothers, is now in the position of prime minister in Egypt and has the power to destroy those who "ruined" his life years before. This chapter chronicles the amazing heart Joseph had to cover his brothers.

Then Joseph could not restrain himself before all those who stood by him, and he cried out, "make everyone go out from me!" So no one stood with him while Joseph made himself known to his brothers. (Genesis 45:1)

The first covering principle we glean from Joseph is this: he did not let anyone uninvolved know the extent of how his brothers had ruined his life. Joseph was a hero in Egypt. The Egyptians were in awe of him as he had saved the entire nation from death. Joseph, now seated in absolute honor in Egypt, did not want anyone to know his brothers crime and risk their honor, and possibly their lives as well. Joseph cleared the room and covered their sin.

To echo R. T. Kendall, who wrote *Total Forgiveness*, by clearing the room, Joseph not only ensured that no one knew the atrocity that had occurred...*Joseph ensured that no one could ever know*. This is exactly how our Father deals with us, and is the heart of true covenant relationships. God confronts us then covers us with his grace and then begins to work on our restoration.

Later in the story, we see how Joseph not only loves his brother's after their offense, but how he covers and restores them. He then offers to provide for them and their posterity with his resources.

"Hurry and go up to my father, and say to him, 'thus says your son Joseph: "God has made me lord of all Egypt; come down to me, do not tarry.10 you shall dwell in the land of Goshen, and you shall be near to me, you and your children, your children's children, your flocks and your herds, and all that you have there will provide for you, lest you and your household, and all that you have, come to poverty; for there are still five years of famine.'" 12 "and behold, your eyes and the eyes of my brother Benjamin see that it is my mouth that speaks to you.13 so you shall tell my father of all my glory in Egypt, and of all that you have seen; and you shall hurry and bring my father down here." 14 then he fell on his brother Benjamin's neck and wept, and Benjamin wept on his neck.15 moreover he kissed all his brothers and wept over them, and after that his brothers talked with him.

Joseph's heart cry is not only to restore his family relationally, but also to bless them abundantly monetarily and cover them with his authority and blessing all the days of their lives. This is covering at its purest and is a model of how wonderful it can be when we enact it through the love descriptions of 1 Corinthians Thirteen.

In many ways Joseph is an Old Testament type of Christ. He was falsely accused, condemned, and then restored to the right hand of Pharaoh. Eventually he was made the head of all authority in his kingdom and showed mercy to those who did not deserve it. Jesus, who now sits at the right hand of God, far above all rule power and dominion, is affording a much greater forgiveness and restoration. Jesus, our covenant maker, covered us in the highest and best example of the concept and desires that you embrace his provision.

I still struggle at times to submit to those who I know only have the best intentions for me, my wife being the first and foremost. Even so, it is the heart of the Father, that we remain as *watchmen* on the spiritual walls for one another, with mutual submission to the Spirit of God found in each of us and spur one another on to his good works.

I pray you will find a place of fellowship that celebrates the gift of who you are, a circle of friends or prayer partners whom you can trust to protect the assignment of God in your life as they challenge you to be all that God intends.

Chapter 9

Your Date is Waiting

For the earnest expectation of the creation, eagerly waits

for the revealing of the sons of God.

(Romans 8:19)

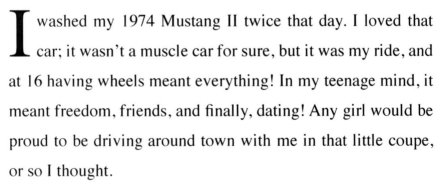

I washed my 1974 Mustang II twice that day. I loved that car; it wasn't a muscle car for sure, but it was my ride, and at 16 having wheels meant everything! In my teenage mind, it meant freedom, friends, and finally, dating! Any girl would be proud to be driving around town with me in that little coupe, or so I thought.

Tired and sunburned after spending the day detailing my pride and joy, I headed for the shower to prepare for my big night. I remember leaving the house with three things: A generous douse of Drakkar cologne, a wad of cash in my pocket totaling sixty dollars, and traces of Turtle Wax® still under my fingernails.

At the tender age of sixteen I was primed for my first date, hoping Robin felt the same. Her smile when she greeted me at the door assured me that she waited with equal anticipation of our exciting night ahead. Her date had arrived!

My friend, ready or not, the world is waiting for us. In Romans 8:19, Paul tells us that not only is she waiting, she is groaning in tumult as she anticipates God's children to appear. The world is pining for someone who looks like Jesus, acts like Jesus, works wonders like Jesus, but most of all, loves like Jesus and can point others to the Father.

The world is waiting on us—you and me. And though we've all been wounded in the battlefield of life, and may have lost our identity and sometimes failed in our mission, yet for all that *we are not*, God still has chosen to rescue the world through you and me.

God has no plan "B." His sons and daughters have too often been content to let local clergy and missionaries abroad be the bearers of light and hope to the world. We allow them to race to fulfill The Great Commission while the rest of us remain in neutral.

The reality is that there is an onus, even a mandate on all of us who have received Christ as savior, to boldly declare his redemption and the Father's love to every nation. We start one heart at a time. As Babbie Mason was inspired to write and sing, "Each one can reach one."

If there has ever been a time for the sons and daughters of the Most High to make themselves known, it is now. America is careening out of control with brokenness and sadly, every city's DHR office has the statistics to prove it. The only remedy is a reconnection with Father God. Once we understand son and daughter-ship and the missional mandate to share our experience, we can walk in the fullness of what that relation-ship affords and requires. There is healing for our brokenness, calmness for our fears, contentment in our situations and con-fidence in our faith.

The Christian life has been called a journey, but to me it's a spiritual quest; a quest to meet the Father and understand my adoption into his family, a quest to know him intimately and live out his purpose for my life. The idea that the God of the universe seeks us out—with all our flaws and stubborn ways—is still amazing to me; even more, that he is forever committed to a desire to live in close fellowship with his children.

As my children began to grow, Lisa suggested I have a "date night" with each one separately. My son and I prefer to call it "guy time," usually working out at the "Y", but my daughters still love date night with dad. Sometimes we go get a burger, or check out the latest Disney movie; other times it's just for yogurt down at Yogurt Mountain, a favorite hangout of ours. Whether it's a trip to somewhere special or just to hang out, their daddy eagerly awaits date night with his kids.

So it is with God.

I hope that this story of my journey has provoked you to rethink your concept of God and the paradigm of what it means to be his child. As we come to the end of our time together, I pray that our Father will continue to reveal himself to you and conform you to the image of Jesus. May this quest infuse your soul with a fierce longing to bring others to the revelation of the wonders of our Abba. May you truly know what it means to be redeemed, reclaimed and restored.

God was there at the beginning of your quest, and he'll be with you all the way until the end. He is our source—where we came from. He is our resource—where we return to again and again for life. Ultimately, he will be our final destination. Please don't wait until you meet him face to face to embrace him for the very first time as *Father*. As Acts 17:28 says, in him we live, move, and have our being—in other words, he is our identity!

I end our visit together with words from A.W. Tozer's work, *The Knowledge of the Holy.*

"What comes into our minds when we think about God is the most important thing about us. For this reason, the gravest question before the Church is always God Himself, and the most portentous fact about any man, is not what he at a given time may say or do, but what he in his deep heart conceives God to be like"[13]

For we have not received the spirit of bondage again to fear;
but ye have received the Spirit of adoption,
whereby we cry Abba, Father.
Romans 8:15

Endnotes

1   Walter Wink, *The Powers That Be: Theology for a New Millennium*. New York: Doubleday, 1999.

2   *Treasury of Spiritual Wisdom*, (compiled by Andy Zubco, San Diego, Blue Dove Press 1998) page 448

3   C.S. Lewis, *The Problem of Pain*, (London: Collins, 1940) page 81

4   James Dobson, *Bringing Up Boys*, (Carol Stream IL, Tyndale House, 2001) page 219

5   Aldous Huxley, Thinkexist.com

6   Jan Coleman, *Woman Behind the Mask* (Grand Rapids, Kregel Publications, 2004) page 66

7   Rick Renner, *Sparkling Gems From The Greek*, (Tulsa Oklahoma, Teach All Nations, 2003) page 525

8   Sermon Illustrations, Our Daily Bread

9   Wikiquote - Field Marshal Ferdinand Foch

10   Steve Brown, *Jumping Hurdles, Hitting Glitches, Overcoming Setbacks*, (Grand Rapids, Baker Book House, 1997) page 164

11   Glen Mackie as quoted in: http://astronomy.swin.edu.au/~gmackie/billions.html

12   Wikiquote – Mohandas Karamchand Gandhi

13   A. W. Tozer, *The Knowledge of the Holy* (New York, 1961), pages 9-10.

CPSIA information can be obtained at www.ICGtesting.com
Printed in the USA
LVOW131826080712

289147LV00001B/56/P